Easy Thai Cooking

75 FAMILY-STYLE DISHES YOU CAN PREPARE IN MINUTES

ROBERT DANHI

foreword by **Corinne Trang**

Photography by **Christian Clements** and **Susie Donald**

Cultural Photography by **Robert Danhi**

TUTTLE Publishing

Tokyo | Rutland, Vermont | Singapore

Snacks on the street packed ready to go

Crispy lime leaves and chilies to nibble on with salad

Hand pounding Tom Yum spice paste

Citrus Sa

Contents

…ispy Shallots

Pad Thai on the streets of Bangkok

A rainbow of curries at Oh Tor Koh Market

Green Papaya Salad Noodle Bowl

Foreword by
Corinne Trang

The cuisine of Thailand remains one of the most popular cuisines in the world. No matter where I've taught or lectured, I've often encountered students who wanted to learn how to cook Thai food. As a result, in my lesson plans, I've always included a popular Thai recipe or two, and now I can recommend to them a cookbook they'll actually use for cooking. *Easy Thai Cooking* by Robert Danhi, includes easy to understand step-by-step simple and delicious recipes for the home cook and professional chef alike. For more than 20 years Robert has traveled back to Thailand, immersing himself in its food culture and bringing back with him a wonderful array of authentic recipes he's recreated in such a way that anyone can grasp. Filled with classics such as Thai Spring Rolls, curries, satays, and Pineapple Fried Jasmine Rice, as well as contemporary recipes such as Red Curry Shrimp Cakes, Sriracha Chicken Salad, and Coriander Beef, *Easy Thai Cooking* is a great illustration of how a classic cuisine inevitably evolves over time, due to trade, tourism, neighboring countries, and any number of factors. For example, my Asian aunts all made spring rolls differently, yet the original family spring roll recipe was my grandmother's. Same source, but different hands and as a result new interpretations! Robert explains from the beginning, how there is not one defining flavor profile that can describe Thailand's food. Rather, like all world cuisines, there are regional differences. Read *Easy Thai Cooking*, follow the recipes, but loosen up in the kitchen, he's giving you the path to authentic Thai flavors and textures as well as the freedom to enjoy the process of cooking by giving you smart shortcuts (like calling for store-bought items such as curry paste, coconut milk, and tamarind concentrate, if you don't feel like making your own from scratch). The chapters are broken down into traditional cookbook chapters, organizing vegetables, fish, and meat into separate chapters, for example, but pay special attention to the chapter entitled "Basic Recipes," which contains a few essential recipes that are at the core of Thai cuisine, such as fried shallots, garlic, and chilies, and a few sauces including homemade Sriracha, if you so desire. I love Robert's loose approach to cooking, always taking into account and respecting Thailand's unique cuisine. The flavors are authentically Thai, yet there is room for experimenting because, as he says, "things ALWAYS change."

Enjoy!

Corinne Trang

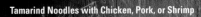
Tamarind Noodles with Chicken, Pork, or Shrimp

Food carts line the streets

Khun Kobkaew, my "ajaan" teacher

Small green and purple eggplants

Forming fre.

My Adventures with Thai Food

My first trip to Southeast Asia came at the relatively young age of nineteen, over 20 years ago, the year prior I had met Estrellita Leong, a beautiful Malaysian woman. We met while taking a cooking class in Los Angeles. We took a journey to visit her family in Malaysia and while we were in the region we visited Thailand. It was immediately apparent that Thailand had a very different food culture. Since then, Thailand's unrestrained range of flavors have delighted my soul.

Once you arrived in the Land of Smiles (as Thailand is called), you know that this is an amazing place, a place where everyone feels welcome. There are endless offerings of food everywhere you look, the lively street corners are active with culinary exchanges, narrow alleyways are packed with people eating, chatting, and playfully laughing about the day's happenings. Open air restaurants churn out plates of addictively spicy cuisine that can be traced to the colorful local markets that supply the country with a bounty of crisp vegetables, aromatic herbs, and fresh seafood.

In the past two decades I have dedicated my life to gaining a better understanding of this region's culinary identity, immersing myself into the traditional food ways that have evolved over the last few thousand years. My first book, *Southeast Asian Flavors* was published with the goal to summarize this dynamic region and give the world a snapshot of the unique cultures of Thailand, Vietnam, Malaysia, and Singapore. This book is different.

What makes this book different?
This book is about everyday cooking for the home cook. Traditional recipes? Not really. Authentic flavors? For sure! My wish is that these recipes become your "go to" recipes for when friends come over for a quick meal, or you need to whip up a weekday dinner, or for a party, or a sit-down meal with the family.

Easy Thai Cooking was created after numerous requests for me to write a book with simpler recipes than *Southeast Asian Flavors*. Frankly, at first I was hesitant to write an "Easy Thai Cookbook." Fearful that I would over simplify recipes that had taken centuries to create. I have too much respect for Thai people and their food culture. Then I started to think about all the food I had eaten in Thailand that were not the iconic dishes that food writers have memorialized in thousands of Thai books, like the *tom yum goong* (hot and sour shrimp soup) and papaya salad (*som tom*), and saw that food evolves and that Thais cook just like us. Not all my meals at home are American classics. People

palm sugar

Lime Cilantro Squid

The markets are filled with smiles

Collecting sap for palm sugar

across the US cook from a similar pantry. So I began to lighten up a bit and think of ways I could create a book with recipes that taste Thai but may not be the traditional versions that I have come to love. Rather, the food I eat when visiting a friend's home in Koh Samui, attending a party in Chiang Mai, or walking down the street late one night in Bangkok discovering a vendor selling their version of fried ramen noodles

I spent countless hours recalling the food I cooked in my home; the recipes I created in my test kitchen; the flavors of Thailand that I fashioned from the condiments on my shelves and from my produce packed refrigerator. I began to realize that the cooking principles I employed in creating dishes that tasted Thai were not really Thai recipes *per se*. There is no one flavor profile that encompasses all of Thailand's food but there are some complex flavors conjured by combining ingredients in balance and employing cooking techniques that produces tastes that are distinctively Thai. It was an "ah-ha" moment, excited that I figured out the focus of the book, I began to pour through my notes, recipe books, thousands of photos, hundreds of videos that I have compiled over the years. I did look at some classic dishes and constructed recipes that pay homage to them but don't quite replicate them.

This was not a new process for me. I taught the culinary arts full time for many years, and while teaching at the Culinary Institute of America in Hyde Park, New York, I had to figure out a way to teach authentic food without over simplifying it. I found myself saying "There are a lot of right ways to make a traditional dish…and there are a few ways to do it wrong." For instance, using heavy cream instead of coconut milk in a Thai curry changes it all together and, in my opinion, it's no longer Thai food. Now, what if I used a premixed curry paste instead? Well, if you go to local markets in Thailand you will see mounds of curry paste waiting to be scooped up and taken home to create an authentic curry. So I began to accept that selecting some key pre-made ingredients could save considerable time and get me closer to creating a simpler recipe for the home cook and still retain the taste of real Thai food.

Some of the recipes that follow I have enjoyed in Thailand, others are renditions of classics that are sure to satisfy, and then there are some recipes that I created. These began with the first step of what I like to call "Cooking on Paper." Step one: decide on a flavor profile that is typically Thai: a salad with a sour-salty and sweet dressing, based on raw ingredients, tossed to order and accented with fresh herbs. Then I look back at the many times I have been to Thailand and try to recall dishes that match that description. Step two: read through the dozens of Thai books I have amassed looking for common threads that run through that style of recipe. Step three: formulate the resulting dish. Using my computer, I used a recipe template, "guesstimating" the ingredient amounts. I would do this for a few weeks, compiling

Ripe red Thai chilies at the market

Cooking with the Karen hill tribe

Khun Posueng and Khun Vorarittinapa grilling satay

Glo

enough recipes to fill a few days of intense cooking. Then I go to the kitchen to try it out, I prepare all the ingredients and keep them measured separately to get a feeling if they are in the right proportions.

I have even developed a technique for what I call "cooking like a chef." Suppose I am making a stir-fry sauce that I can't figure out the exact amount for the ingredients. I weigh each open container and enter this into one column of a spreadsheet, then cook like I normally would: using my heart, hands and mind. Then, after I get the right taste, I weigh these ingredients again and enter them in the next column and it calculates how much I used. Then I convert to volume measures and edit the recipe. I print out this recipe and get everything measured out ahead of time, prepare it as written, and make any necessary adjustments along the way. Even if it comes out perfectly, I always test it one more time. Every time I made the recipe I would ask the same very core question: "Does this taste Thai?"

So there you have it, simple recipes that have an authentic taste but may not be a traditional recipes.

A Snapshot of Traditional Thai Culture

Many factors influence and create the characteristics of a culture. It all begins with the geography. Thailand is situated in between Myanmar (Burma), Laos, Cambodia, and Malaysia. Most of the country is situated between 10° and 20° latitude in the north-ern hemisphere and its vast landscape enables a wide variety of crops to be grown and animals to be raised. The extensive river network is ideal for aquaculture. The Gulf of Thailand and Andaman Sea provides access to the ocean's bounty and bustling ports for import and exportation, allowing Thailand to become a significant player in the food manufacturing world.

Unlike its surrounding neighbors, Thailand has never been colonized and so it seems to readily absorb foreign influences. A large majority of Thais are Buddhist and hence a spiritual approach to even the most mundane tasks is commonplace. All young males take their turns at becoming a monk. The sages roam the streets to collect food that is donated by average citizens, it is an honor to do so and these morsels of food sustain them each and every day.

The Thai spirit is truly special, they try to have fun in everything they do, actually they have a word for this, *sanuk*. It's a much more casual social setting than any of the adjacent countries. Thais wearing shorts and t-shirts is commonplace. However, the contrasting opposite is the formality seen each Monday where most of the population wears yellow clothing to honor the king, many with the king's official crest affixed to the outfit. Anytime they pass a photo or statue of the king they *wai*, this gesture of putting both hands together with a modest bow is a sign of respect, especially to elders. Just as with most of Asian cultures, "saving face" is very important, it is improper etiquette to embarrass yourself or others in public.

...th woven into garland

Fresh Sweet Pineapple with Chili Salt

Miang Khum "Explosive Bites" street hawker

Thais are like family

Another regional practice, specific to Southeast Asia, is not eating as often with chopsticks and more so with the combination of a spoon and fork. Once you try eating this way you will never go back. The spoon is held in your dominant hand and the fork is in the other hand pushing some rice, a bit of sauce and maybe a few stray bits of chilies onto the spoon. Yes, chopsticks are used here, but mostly for noodle dishes and often in conjunction with a spoon in the other hand to scoop up the soup or sauce.

Thais possess an aesthetic for their food. Much of this may very well have evolved 700 years ago from Sukhothai, the capital of Thailand. The king was adamant that special attention and training was given to the artful presentation of food and ornate carving of fruits and vegetables. To this day, carved cucumber leaves may be used to scoop up a Thai chili dip, national food carving happen thoroughly out the year and an overall attention to details can be seen across every socio-economic group and region in Thailand.

Street food sustains today's modern busy city dwellers, many of these foods are one bowl meals meant to be eaten individually. More formal meals consist of a selection of dishes. Usually no special order is followed. At Thai homes, dishes are cooked and sit out at room temperature (in the tropics things stay relatively warm) and all are eaten at once. Relax and go with the flow!

Table condiments are a big deal in Southeast Asia, and Thailand is no exception. Most Thai tables have a few small jars filled with seasonings that each person can use according to their preference. The most common is a small jar filled with chopped Thai chilies covered with fish sauce, this gives you a burst of sodium along with a bit of spice. Ground roasted dry chilies are sprinkled on noodles, and often balanced with another table seasoning: granulated sugar. Other forms of heat like Sriracha chili sauce, and various others that don't have international status because they are created by individual street hawkers, restaurant cooks, and fine dining restaurant chefs.

Yes, there is a vibrant dining scene in Thailand and major cities like Bangkok are packed with posh dining establishments or Thai food and other international cuisines. All the multi-national hotel chains have numerous restaurants, and there are culinary schools that teach the traditional and modern art of Thai food.

Get in Your Kitchen and Cook!

This book is here to guide you as you explore the fabulous tastes of Thailand. If you need it, I have videos and photos to lead you step-by-step in the kitchen and give you insight into the nuances that will help you create really special Thai food and drinks (chefdanhi.com).

Haven't been to Thailand? Start planning now. In the meantime I want to share my experiences with you. Within the pages of this book I have hopefully provided you with enough information to get you on the right track creating the flavors of Thailand in your own kitchen. If you need help, reach out and I am here. Go to chefdanhi.com for contact information.

Stocking Your Thai Pantry

My goal in this chapter is to demystify the ingredients used within this book. Enabling you to find these building blocks of flavor at your local grocer or order them online. Once you know what to look for, discover how they are commonly used, and learn the basics for storage you are well on your way to creating the authentic flavors of Thailand in your kitchen.

The following pages will lead you through the basic ingredients, however, the quality and overall flavor variation between different growers, manufacturers, importers, and distributors is enormous, so knowing what to look for is essential in finding the most appropriate ingredient. Cooking the foods of Southeast Asia for the past two decades I have discovered, tasted, experimented with and, sometimes, discarded thousands of things. What was once my favorite brand is replaced by another one years later and other items, like rice powder already roasted and ground, I could not find even five years ago is now in most markets I frequent. It is an evolving landscape and is why I created chefdanhi.com, to constantly keep you informed of the latest and greatest building blocks of Thai flavor. There are links there for finding your closest market stocked with Asian ingredients.

Stocking your kitchen puts you in control and only a few items need to be bought fresh. Storing these building blocks of flavor in your pantry, refrigerator, and freezer allowing you to whip up a meal at a moment's notice. The freezer will extend the shelf life of some key ingredients. Buy and store some of these items for when you are in need. Some things such as banana leaves, lime leaves, chilies, shrimp, minced lemongrass can be bought and immediately stored in the freezer. The same goes for seeds, nuts, fried shallots, garlic, and dried shrimp.

Sometimes I like to get ahead and prepare some things before freezing. Peeled galangal and ginger hold up well, I simply grate them when frozen or slice a few pieces as needed. I even have minced lemongrass in bulk, and spread onto a baking sheet to freeze (freeze in small particles) then gather up into a bag or container so I can scoop them out and cook later—about 1 tablespoon minced lemongrass per stalk. If I have extra fresh squeezed lime juice, I portion into small containers, or an ice cube tray, freeze and pull out what I need. If you want to make your own curry pastes, look to my *Southeast Asian Flavors* book for the recipes, you can make the paste and freeze in portions for later reference.

In Thailand, most condiments and spice pastes are stored at room temperature, however they often consume these items more quickly than Westerners. Hence, storing some items in the refrigerator makes them last longer. Chili sauces, curry pastes, seafood condiments (fish sauce, oyster sauce), and tamarind paste can be chilled for maximum quality retention.

Fresh vegetables, fruits, herbs, meat, and seafood must be bought when you need them. Getting to know your local store's staff will surely help you glean the most select cuts of meat, fresh fish, and produce. Take the time to establish these relationships and you will be rewarded with the things you need to create truly delicious Thai flavors. I sometimes even bring samples of the food I make—keeping the staff happy means they will look out for quality ingredients for my Thai meal.

Bok choy   **Choy sum**   **Water spinach**

Asian Greens It almost pains me to group such a diverse family of vegetables into one category. The various deep green versions of bok choy, choy sum, water spinach, or flowering broccoli of the *brassica* family can be used in the recipes, use your judgment pairing heartier greens with bold flavored recipes. Firm, perky leaves and stems without any discoloration on the cut stem side are sure signs of freshness. Keep these covered to avoid wilting from dehydration.

Bean Sprouts Made from sprouting the small green mung beans. Fastidious cooks pick off the straggly ends one by one, leaving the sweetest pearly, white crunchy small stalks for adding texture to salads, noodle bowls and stir-fries. Avoid brown, wilted, or slimily wet sprouts. Handle them gently and keep them in an air tight bag or container for a couple of days.

Dried chilies

Finger length chilies

Thai chilies

Chilies The Thai people's passion and copious use of chilies is profound. The recipes in this book primarily use two chilies: the intensely spicy small **Thai chili** and the more mild, yet still hot, finger-length red chilies. These chilies are pounded, sliced thinly,

minced, crushed or left whole for a gentle infusion. The capsaicin compound responsible for the spice is primarily located in the veins, seeds are guilty by close association and the rest of the chili has some heat (see "Working with Chilies," page 25). They should be firm, dark green to red and not shriveled and black. The best substitute is frozen Thai chilies, available in freezer section or just freeze fresh ones when available. You can substitute with Serrano. For the finger-length red chilies you could use jalapenos but I prefer the ripe red Fresno chilies.

Dried Chilies When chilies are dried their taste evolves since the drying process is slow they slightly ferment and concentrate, and achieve a deep red color. Water soaked chilies are often pounded or ground into spice pastes, marinades, and dressings. Also found on the table as a condiment, the dried chilies are roasted and ground. They can also be quickly fried whole and used as a spicy and crispy edible accompaniments to a variety of salads and other dishes.

Chili Paste in Soya Bean Oil (Nahm Prik Pow) Flavorful concoction of deep roasted-slightly sweet flavor comes from fried garlic and shallots, chilies, and dried shrimp. Palm sugar and tamarind balance the flavor and creates this multi-purpose sauce used in many of the recipes in this book. The base of a quick hot and sour soup (see Hot and Sour Tamarind Soup, page 56), component of a glaze (Grilled Chicken Wings with Tangy Chili Glaze, page 46), or simply spread on bread with a few slices of cucumber as a snack this is one of my favorite ingredients. This complex sauce is not easily duplicated and this ingredient tends to hold a pivotal role in the recipes it resides in. If a store-bought product cannot be found, you can make it yourself (see Thai Chili Jam, page 36). Once a container is open it keep in the refrigerator for months.

Cinnamon (Cassia) The dried bark of two varieties of trees, is infused in savory stews and broths and is part of the famous Chinese five spice used throughout Asia. The thicker bark, known as cassia is most common in Asia, yet the thinner type is acceptable in smaller amounts. Rather than grinding to a powder, it is common to use whole strips to infuse a soup or sauce. The two different types of this spice do not need to be labeled differently so follow the aforementioned visual clues and try to find the thicker cassia at an Asian market or online.

Coriander Leaves (Cilantro) The leafy green herb from which the coriander seed is produced has an amazing flavor all its own. Possessing a lemony, floral aroma and sharp tartness on the palate. As the most widely used herb in Southeast Asia all parts of this plant are very useful. The leaves and tender stems are usually chopped together, the seeds are used as a spice (Coriander Beef, Page 69), and roots have an earthy flavor used in most curry pastes and many marinades.

Coriander Seeds These seeds emerge from the top of the coriander (cilantro) plant at maturity. Their strong earthy and lemon-like flavor is ground into spice pastes. Toast seeds until slightly darkened, let cool, then, if need be, grind. There is no substitute, you might want to try to use fresh coriander leaves (cilantro).

Fresh Coconuts Coconuts change as they mature, young green-skinned ones are packed with juice (referred to as coconut water) and the flesh is soft and gelatinous. The older they get the thicker, and firmer and rich with fat that provides coconut milk, a pillar of Thai cooking. Cracking open a coconut requires a few swift swings of a large knife. Buying fresh coconuts can be

challenging, many stores have inventory that sit for a long time and go sour, so seek out a reliable supplier. Young coconut juice/water can be bought canned, actually some brands are quite tasty. The frozen plastic containers have the best flavor and still somewhat silky flesh. Mature coconut should be heavy with juice, give a shake to feel for this and listen.

Coconut Milk and Cream Decadent white liquid with a hint of sweetness and velvetly smooth texture. Made by taking the shredded hard white flesh of mature coconuts, blended with water and squeezed to yield opulent creamy fluid. Coconut cream on the other hand is traditionally made by squeezing the shredded meat without water, then the water is added for a second extract on coconut milk. To learn more about making your own fresh coconut milk look in *Southeast Asian Flavors* or chefdanhi.com. Coconut milk is used as a foundation for savory curries, to enrich soups and sauces and create decadent sweet treats.

Canned or boxed coconut milk is pasteurized, often homogenized and sometimes stabilized; making the milk thicker than hand-made. To keep it simple this book was developed using all canned/boxed milk.

Squeezing the shredded meat without water traditionally makes coconut cream, then the water is added for a second extract on coconut milk. Used to begin Thai curries (see pages 28–29), for coconut toppings and custards and other places the rich satisfying cream is appropriate. Coconut milk should have about 15–23% fat content. Coconut cream contains about 24% fat.

Eggplant There are dozens of varieties commonly used in Asia, in Thailand some common varieties include the round (1½–2 inch /4–5 cm) diameter variegated green orbs, or the long slender purple Chinese/Japanese varieties. The variegated green are used raw to scoop up spicy chili dips or simmered in green curries, where as the longer eggplants are usually cooked. Firm fleshed, smooth skin with firm stems should be present. Store loosely covered in the refrigerator.

Fried Garlic and Shallots These two favorite flavor boosters have become staples in kitchens across all of Southeast Asia. Although browned garlic and shallots can be created as the first stage of cooking a recipe, these crispy versions are used at the last moment, adding a crunch, a rich flavor and appealing look. You can make your own

(see Fried Garlic, page 37 and Fried Shallots page 37). Bags, jars or plastic containers are available—the quality varies greatly. I look for those that only list shallot or garlic and oil, those with palm oil tend to have the best crunch and overall flavor. Avoid those that have flour or other starches included. They keep for months in the freezer or even the refrigerator where I keep a jar with a shake top for quick reference. They can be left at room temperature for weeks, I use my home made versions at room temperature. If they are store-bought, I store them frozen and defrost when needed.

Fish Sauce This salty, pungent, and essential seasoning has an amber color, and substantial umami impact, rounding out a lot of flavorful Thai foods. It is often the major sodium source in Thai food. Cooking a majority of real Thai food for vegetarians is a challenge since fish sauce is used so often, I turn to light soy sauce or low-sodium soy sauce and begin with the same amount. If you don't use it often you may want to keep in your refrigerator to slow down the aging process. Sometimes sodium crystals form in the bottle over extended times, no need to worry, proceed on!

Galangal (blue ginger) (Kha) Much tougher than ginger, the readily apparent lines around its circumference of the thin skin encompasses a mustard-camphor like citrusy aroma. I like to keep them loosely wrapped in the refrigerator. If they are hard for you to find (or order online), peel and freeze a large piece (you can find it in many freezer sections at markets also). When in need, grate it frozen so you can measure them easily or slice off a few pieces. Dried powder or slices have no flavor, better to use nothing or substitute with ginger.

Green Papaya Actually an immature, not just unripe papaya, is firm and really not that flavorful, it's a textural experience and a medium for seasonings. Look for smooth green skins without wrinkles. The surface should be very firm, almost hard. Store loosely covered or in a drawer in the refrigerator.

Kaffir Lime Leaves and Zest This aromatic branch of the citrus family tree is prized mostly for its pungent leaves. The wrinkly fruit has a wonderfully strong scented zest used in spice pastes but the juice of the fruit is almost never used. Leaves are steeped whole in broths and curries, fried quickly to a crisp for snacks or garnish. Look for the uniquely double lobed sturdy leaves that are shiny and dark green on one side and a matte light green on the other. For every 6 lime leaves I use 1 teaspoon lime zest, usually added towards the end of the recipe. Best when fresh, useless when dried. They freeze quite well, make sure to keep them airtight and only pull out those needed for each recipe.

Lemongrass These sturdy slender stalks are an icon for Thai food. It has a crisp citrus aroma that perfumes Thai dishes at all ends of the spectrum from cool salads to fiery hot curries. Most commonly, the bottom 4–6 inches (10–15 cm) are used for infusing, mincing, or slicing very thinly to shorten the tough fibers that run lengthwise. The outer tougher leaves must be stripped away, revealing the aromatic and tender inside. As a substitute I would suggest ½ teaspoon lemon zest with ¼ teaspoon lime zest for each stalk of lemongrass. Better yet, buy frozen already chopped lemongrass or buy fresh stalks when available and freeze them for future use. Keep them, wrapped loosely, in the refrigerator for a week or two.

Limes Limes and all citrus are indigenous to the Asian continent. There are a variety of limes used in Thai cuisine including the largest Persian lime or common lime, small "key" lime, knobby kaffir lime, and the perfumed kalamansi lime. This book only utilizes the most common limes. In Thai cuisine, the juice is commonly used in uncooked recipes for dressing and as a final tableside garnish, the flavor does not hold up well under heat or over time, so juice your limes as you need them. Never buy bottled lime juice. The zest is grated when the aroma of the lime is what you want, the oils contain most of the precious aroma. Look for bright or dark green limes that are firm to the touch without any brown or soft spots. They can be kept room temperature for a few days, but I keep them loosely covered in the refrigerator.

Long Beans (Yard Beans) Heartier than standard green beans these earthy tasting beans are 1–2 feet long (about ½ meter). Snacked on raw as part of a table salad to accompany salads and rice dishes or cooked, these are flavorsome beans. I prefer the deep green variety. The stem end should not be dried out and shriveled. Store covered loosely in the refrigerator.

Mint (Peppermint) Mint's unique ability to produce a refreshing cooling sensation gives it a star role in the Southeast Asia. It may pack a wallop of flavor yet extensive exposure to heat kills its flavor so it's usually eaten raw or added at the very last moment. There are two primary varieties: peppermint (more commonly used), which has wrinkled leaves and hard woody stems; while spearmint has smooth darker green leaves and soft edible stems and has a more assertive bite—same as Thai basil.

Dried flat rice noodles

Dried rice vermicelli noodles

Fresh flat rice noodlers

Dried bean thread noodles
(Cellophane noodles, Glass noodles)

Noodles, Dried Flat Rice Probably the most popular noodle in Thailand, these noodles come in many sizes, as thin as ⅛ inch (3 mm) and as wide as ¾ inch (2 cm). Transform these noodles into soups and stir-fried dishes. Soak for 30 minutes in room temperature water before a quick boil. More often than not dried noodles will be labeled with the Vietnamese "Banh Pho." Store at room temperature, sealed air tight—almost indefinitely.

Dried Rice Vermicelli Noodles (Rice Sticks) The thinnest of all rice noodles, they have a subtle flavor and delicate texture. In Thailand there is one special variety known as *Khanom Jin*—the batter is slightly fermented before making noodles. Salads, noodle bowls, soups,

and stir-fried dishes all welcome these firm threads that act as flavor carriers. I prefer to soak them in water first, then boiled to cook for the best texture. I look for ingredient statements that list only rice and water (maybe salt). Recently some manufacturers have been adding tapioca starch, making them more durable but creating a different texture.

Fresh Flat Rice Noodles The Chinese invented the technique of making a thin batter of ground rice or rice flour batter that's steamed into sheets then cut into various widths. Once refrigerated they get brittle, so buy them, take them home, and pull into individual noodles, then gather up and refrigerate in portions. They are often sold on a shelf in a non-refrigerated section of the market.

Look for markets that have daily deliveries of these supple ribbons. It's okay to buy at room temperature and use that same day, then keep in the refrigerator for up to a week, they are vastly superior on the first day.

Dried Bean Thread Noodles (Cellophane Noodles, Glass Noodles) Skinny, transparent noodles made from the starch of mung beans. Little flavor to speak of but with a resilient texture. They are used in salads, soups, and spring rolls. Simply cooked by covering dried noodles in boiling water for about 5 minutes and then draining.

Oyster Sauce This Asian food essential was invented in China in 1888 by Lee Kum Kee, in one of history's finest accidents. A pot of oyster stew was forgotten, it boiled down into this enchantingly heady nectar. Now used across Asia, this culinary powerhouse is deep brown with hues of gold and has a potent salty, slightly sweet, seafood flavor. Flavor from oyster extract, slightly sweet with sugar, seasoned with salt, and thickened with starch, it has the unique ability to not only season, but tenderize marinated meats and seafood. It also can give a distinctive sheen to sauces and glazed items. The more oyster extractives the better—higher priced bottles are often an indication of this desirable quality trait. For those with diets that exclude oysters, look for "vegetarian oyster or stir-fry sauce" that can be used as a substitute, using equal amounts.

Pandanus leaves Long slender deep green leaves contain the most charming aroma due to the natural presence of 2-Acetyl-1-pyrroline. Any green sweet in Thailand is bound to be colored and aromatically infused with this special herb. There is no substitute, vanilla added to a recipe that calls for pandanus may taste good but will not taste Thai. I buy fresh when it's available,

and freeze some when I get home or I buy frozen leaves. Always trim the lighter colored bottom portion (it tastes like dirt). Keep fresh, wrapped tightly in the refrigerator for a few days, frozen they keep for months.

Peppercorns True peppercorns created the primary spicy sensation across Asia before chilies arrived in the 15th century. The same plant is processed into three colors: green peppercorns are picked immature and usually pickled; black are produced by fermenting and drying green ones; white are soaked, husked, and sun dried. Whole black peppercorns can be used to infuse; coarsely crushed they add bursts of fiery bites; white pepper is generally ground finest, added to spice pastes or added at the very end of cooking. Green peppercorns are usually used whole. Thai cooks use each colored peppercorn separately and don't buy mixtures. Green ones are rarely found fresh outside of Asia. I buy them brined in salted water (avoid vinegar). Black and white are both sold dried. Look for plump, somewhat evenly colored white and evenly shaped shriveled black peppercorns.

Peanuts (Groundnuts) An icon for Southeast Asian cuisine, peanuts are included on all parts of the menu. Creamy peanut sauce, pan-roasted, crushed, and tossed into noodles or transformed into a sweet filling for a sweet snack, the peanut's versatility is unmatched. Roasting your own peanuts has its flavorful rewards. Slowly pan roasting or a quick deep-frying are best. Some shelled peanuts still have the skin attached, they are delicious if not a bit messy to peel so you may want to get peeled raw nuts and roast them yourself. If you do choose to save time

by buying them pre-roasted then make sure they are unsalted and un-seasoned. Keep in the freezer to extend their life to 6 months.

Pork Fat This is a common cooking ingredient. The flavor elements it contributes and the texture it creates is unmatched. Thais like to deep-fry, pan-fry, or stir-fry in rendered pork fat. You can buy what is labeled as lard—a somewhat neutral flavored pork fat. It does have more flavor and a thicker mouth feel than vegetable oil and, for some stir-fries, I like this.

Jasmine Rice Uniquely aromatic rice naturally contains aromatic compound called 2-Acetyl-1-pyrroline. Commonly called steamed rice by mistake it is cooked by covering with water and bringing it to a boil. Jasmine rice that's grown in Thailand is government authorized to be labeled as Thai Ho Mali, it is quite special. This species, however, is grown around the globe, even in California, with great results.

Sticky Rice A long grain rice packed with a unique starch structure that gives the cooked rice a firm and elastic texture. A staple of northern Thailand, usually soaked then steamed. Used in sweets, toasted and ground as a flavorful thickener and used to scoop up sauce and salads. Look for the stark long-grain white rice often labeled as glutinous or sweet rice. There is no true substitute, regular long grain rice can be served as a side instead. Store at room temperature, sealed air tight—almost indefinitely.

Salt In the USA, most cooks and chefs prefer kosher salt. Most sea salt is also not overly processed, and available globally, so that is another salt you can use. The size of the grain actually can make a significant difference in measuring salt. Since salt is not used too much in the book (sodium is usually added in the form of fish sauce, soy sauce, or ready-made condiments) and in small amount it won't make much of a difference. Start with less and add more as needed. If you only have iodized fine table salt reduce the amount by half, taste, and adjust from there.

Soy Sauce Dried soy beans are soaked, cooked, and inoculated with special mold and fermented for months, during this process the proteins are naturally broken down to free glutamate and increase in savory flavor—the same thing that happens with fish sauce. Soy sauce is used less frequently than fish sauce but similarly. Used to add a depth of flavor by adding sodium and its unique taste. Each soy sauce, like wine, can be made from the same primary ingredient, yet can taste drastically different. Look for naturally "brewed," actually a term used to designate that this was fermented during an extended aging process giving it a rich flavor and dark color. Do not buy brands that contain caramel coloring (except for dark soy sauce where caramel coloring is acceptable).

Sriracha Sauce Invented in its namesake town of Sriracha, Thailand, a southern seaport village just North of Pattaya, this traditionally fermented chili sauce was originally a table condiment, but its popularity has made it into the ingredient list of many modern dishes. Mostly chilies, garlic, vinegar, sugar, salt, and vinegar. I have used it as a primary seasoning in salads and noodles. There are many different brands of this beloved condiment each with its own style. Other fine pureed chili sauces from places like Singapore, Malaysia, and Vietnam may work but a taste test is the only real gauge. Once a container is open it keeps in the refrigerator for months.

Star Anise Shaped like an eight-pointed star, hence the name, the flavor of black licorice or fennel. A key ingredient of Chinese five spices. This spice is steeped in aromatic stews and soups as well as ground into a variety of spice blends and pastes. Make sure to remove it before serving a dish (one bite is a definite turn off).

Stocks and Broths Stocks are made primarily of bones while broths include meat. General purpose Asian style stocks are more subtle than their western cousins of the same name because they are not made with the tradi-tional combination of bones, carrot, onion, celery, and aromatics. Usually they just have bones, meat, or shells and a couple of aromatics infused in simmering water. Chicken, pork, shrimp, fish, and beef stocks are also utilized in Thai cuisine. These form the basis of many Thai soups and help add moisture to stir-fried dishes. Canned or boxed broths or stocks can be substituted with decent result. I actually suggest adding some water (up to an equal amount) to create a neutral flavored all-purpose stock. Let taste be your guide. Look for reduced sodium labels as they allow for better control of seasoning. If you make a fresh stock, cool it quickly and store in refrigerator for about a week. It's best to freeze it for longer storage, up to a few months is fine. Canned or boxed items can be stored at room temperature, once opened, transfer to new container and store in the refrigerator for about a week.

Sweetened Condensed Milk A luxurious milk creation, pearly white and strikingly sweet (45% sugar) it is rich, viscous, and delicious. Created in the late 1800's by concentrating fresh milk and adding loads of sugar. The not-so-secret, yet ever so magical sweet-ener calms the intense Thai Iced Coffee (page 114). I find it is also very handy to enrich sweets, such as the Grilled Bananas with Sesame Seeds (page 108). Beware of less expensive cans labeled as "Sweetened Condensed Filled Milk" as they are cut with hydrogenated vegetable fat. Nothing com-pares or can be substituted. Evaporated milk is used for Thai tea and is similarly concen-trated, yet no sugar is added. Once opened, transfer to a new container, cover, and store in the refrigerator for up to a few weeks.

Sweet Soy Sauce Much darker, thicker, and sweeter than regular soy sauce with a flavor similar to salty molasses. Used in meat marinades as a tenderizing flavor enhancer and seasoning element. Some Thai brands are labeled as Thai Sweet Sauce. An acceptable substitute is the thicker Indonesian Kecap Manis.

Tamarind Concentrate Large fruit pods, filled with a deep brown, sticky, tart-n-sweet paste hang from trees. (To make your own paste go to page 25.) The paste is processed into blocks that are sold to be diluted with water to form a pulp. However, for convenience, you can find ready-made concentrates. All recipes in this book can be made with the concentrate. Soups are soured, sauces are balanced, glazes are thickened and drinks are made refreshing with tamarind. Look for ingredient labels with a short ingredient list with tamarind

listed first. Although sodium is not listed on the ingredient statement, they can be salty, containing around 3% sodium. The paste can be stored at room temperature, the pre-made concentrate must be stored in refrigerator once opened. The paste lasts for more than 6 months, an open concentrate will last for a month.

Thai Basil (Asian Basil) Probably the most common herb in Thai cooking, it's easily recognized by its smooth pointed leaves attached to a purple stem. The flavor is similar to common basil with scents of anise and cinnamon. It is used as a raw garnish as well as added at the end (in copious amounts) wilting and reserving the color and perfuming the entire dish. Curries, soups and salads all welcome its flavor. The anise-like aroma that these possess is tough to duplicate, if Thai basil can't be found, simply use equivalent amounts of the common basil. Sometimes I add a small pinch of finely ground star anise or anise. Look for unblemished leaves that are firm and deep green. Fresh herbs are very perishable—heat, physical abuse, and moisture need to be managed. I have found that gently and loosely wrapping the bunch in paper towels then placing in seal bag and storing in the refrigerator keeps them fresh the longest—up to a week.

Thai Curry Pastes Wet spice pastes are created by grinding aromatics, such as fresh coriander leaves (cilantro), lemongrass, galangal, kaffir lime leaves, garlic, and shallots. Also roasted and pulverized spices like coriander, cumin, and peppercorns are traditionally pounded in stone mortars with a pestle. Electric powered mechanical devices such as blenders and food processors are now commonly used. Curry pastes are rarely used raw, they are most often fried in coconut oil. Recently I have been experimenting using the typical red, green, yellow, mussaman, penang curry pastes that I make or buy already prepared in non traditional recipes. The Crunchy Sweet Papaya Pickles (page 42) dish is a result of this. Most stores stock curry pastes on the dry goods shelves in bags, plastic tubs, or cans. Once a container is open it keeps in the refrigerator for months.

Thai Palm Sugar (Coconut Sugar) Golden brown to light tan in color and sweet like granulated sugar with a hint of caramel. Made by boiling the sap of a palm tree (sometimes a coconut palm) down to a syrup, then crystallized into a sugar. Not only is it sweet, it really has a notable flavor, used to sweeten and enhance a dish, sweet or savory. Formed into disks, ranging from 2–6 inch (5–30 cm) or packed in plastic

Firm tofu   **Pressed tofu**   **Silken tofu**

Tofu (Bean Curd) Entire books are and should be dedicated to the vast array of soybean protein based tofu. In Thailand they use most major varieties of tofu, such as curd, silken, sheets, and fried. This books uses silken tofu that is gelatinized soy milk, making it silky smooth. Silken tofu is sold in aseptic-boxes—no refrigeration is needed and curd tofu is sold fresh, basking in water. Once fresh tofu is opened it needs to be used within a few days.

spice imparts its color to just about anything, including fingers (some people wear gloves when handling turmeric). It is used to tint curries, marinated meats, and even tofu throughout the region (Grilled Tofu Curry, page 85). Purchase turmeric in its powder form as the dried whole rhizomes are hard to use and have no real benefit to them. Fresh turmeric is becoming more common and it has a different taste and strength. For every 1 teaspoon of dried I use 1 tablespoon (½ oz/14 g) of fresh grated.

containers. Pay close attention to the color as there are several varieties of palm sugar distinguishable only by flavor and color. Thai style (as is Vietnamese) palm sugar is light brown whereas palm sugar from Malaysia or Indonesia is dark brown and should not be used as a substitute. Light brown sugar is the best substitute. Keep in an airtight container at room temperature. When you bring some home from the market, use a hand grater or set up your food processor with grating/shredding attachment and grate all the sugar, store in a covered plastic container and scoop it out when you need it.

Thai Sweet Chili Sauce Hailing from the northern region of Issan, and traditionally served with Gai Yaang (a spice marinated grilled chicken) its sweet syrupy texture is speckled with chili flakes and garlic yielding a mostly sweet and slightly sour mildly spicy sauce. It's commonly used as a dipping sauce straight from the bottle. It's easy to

make your own (see Thai Sweet Chili Sauce, page 35). If I buy it, I usually fortify it with some chopped coriander leaves (cilantro), minced ginger, and add a touch of fish sauce or soy sauce to calm the sweetness. I also like using it to glaze grilled ribs (see Sweet-n-Spicy Pork Ribs, page 47). Once a container is open it keeps in the refrigerator for months.

Turmeric Powder The dried rhizome that is ground into a fine powder. utilized primarily for its bright orange-yellow color rather than its subdued almost chalky taste. This

Yellow Bean Sauce (Yellow Bean Paste, Brown Bean Sauce) Deep brown in color, this thick salty paste is made from ground and fermented soybeans. Packing a sodium and umami laden punch it provides a depth of flavor. Fermented and salted yellow soy beans can be chopped or mashed. This flavorful paste is a byproduct of soy sauce production. Store in the refrigerator for up to a couple of months.

Thai Cooking Tips

Cooking is easy. Yet, superior cooking requires paying attention to each and every step in the process. If you have been cooking for a long time, you unconsciously have already made hundreds of decisions every time you are in the kitchen. This does not require more cooking time, in fact it is easier and more enjoyable, especially once you get a grasp on the fundamental techniques used to create the authentic tastes of any region and Thai food is no different. Once you master the basics, you can modify recipes and create your own dishes with ease. The first stage of a recipe often requires some preparation of the raw ingredients. In the following section you will find some of the most common techniques explained. Once you get everything prepped, then it's time to cook.

Recipes are merely guidelines. The variance of the raw ingredients and the use of different equipment requires adaptation to the changing situation in the kitchen. Sometimes it's good to get ahead. I have provided you with tips for preparing lemongrass, chilies, rhizomes, and peanuts. All of these actually freeze rather well, nothing tastes like fresh, but depending on your location this may be the difference of making something with what you have stored away or not making it at all.

For the lemongrass, chilies, rhizomes, if they are whole, I peel them first and place in a thick, air-tight plastic resealable bag. When I need some, I pull it out and cut it as needed otherwise using a rasp or other grater to grate off exactly what I need. When you have already prepared them I suggest you spread them out on a baking sheet, then freeze. This keeps the individual piece separate, once frozen, gather up quickly (avoid defrosting) and re-freeze in a bag, allowing you to easily retrieve what you need, when you need it.

I recommend that you read the recipe first, you may even want to follow it the first time you make it. Take the time to read through the recipe, a couple of times if possible. I gather everything I am going to use and get organized. Take a few minutes now, it will make cooking easier and more enjoyable.

What stove do you have? All the recipes in the book were tested extensively on a standard gas range. The traditional recipes were adapted to work at home. Electric ranges can be used, frankly a electric cook-top can often have more heat than a gas home range, but the big down fall is the lack of response (delayed really) making cooking on these difficult. When you need to begin on high heat and then lower it quickly, I turn on two burners—one high and one low so I can move the pan when I need to "lower the heat" immediately.

Can you spell Thai? Since the Thai language is not based on the Roman alphabet, translating into the written English language gives way to numerous spellings for recipes and ingredients alike. There may be a government standard but ingredient labels, menus, books, and website spellings vary, keep alert so you can recognize the recipe or ingredient.

I have given you weights (in grams) for any dry ingredients with a ¼ cup or more per recipe. Depending on how you pack a measuring cup with basil the amount can vary greatly. (A cup of basil averages 25 grams but when testing the recipe we had as little as 30 grams and as much as 40 grams) Don't worry about it, it's cooking after all, use what you feel is correct, you can always add more!

Preparing Ginger and Galangal

These underground stems are very fibrous and hence may need to be cut a certain way to ensure the best texture for your recipes. Whether they are whole or prepared already, you can freeze these successfully.

Peeling First: I like to use the edge of a spoon to scrape away the peel.

Slicing: Large wafers can infuse broths and curries. I recommend cutting them into ⅛ inch (3 mm) thick to extract the maximum flavor and still thick enough to pull them out later.

Mincing: Trim off one edge creating a flat surface to stand it up on, slice large thin slabs ¹⁄₁₆–⅛ inch (1–3 mm). Restack these up, then cut into very thin, ¹⁄₁₆–⅛ inch (1–3 mm) strips, gather these up, turn them 90 degrees and cut across. Then cut each half lengthwise into fine long strips. Turn these 90 degrees and cut perpendicular (⅛ inch/3 mm) to create a minced ginger. Then cut back and forth a few times to make sure it is all cut evenly.

Preparing Lemongrass

Usually store-bought lemongrass has the long leaves trimmed from the top. The hearty stalk's bottom 4–6 inches (10–15 cm) is the most tender and aromatic and they are the part most often used in cooking.

1 Cut off the tops, discarding the discolored layers. Save the tops for another use such as the Lemongrass Iced Tea (page 115) or add a few of these to a simmering stock. I keep a re-sealable plastic bag in the freezer and add a few at a time as I cook, then occasionally I need them when fresh is not available or I may make some iced tea.

2 Trim off the discolored bottom of the root end, then peel off any discolored outer layers, I usually take off at least one of the older outer layers that has been exposed to other shoppers' hands and is probably dehydrated anyway.

3 The next step is determined on what you want to do with the lemongrass.

Thinly sliced to be used as is or ground into paste: Carefully cut the trimmed stalk in half lengthwise, then cut off the hard core at the bottom. It does not taste good, certainly not like the rest of the stalk so I generally cut it out. Turn halves 90 degrees and cut perpen-

dicular very thinly (⅛ inch/3 mm maximum), creating crescent-shaped slices.

Bruised for infusion: Use a blunt object to bruise the stalk (the back of a knife works fine), bruise just enough for the liquid to penetrate and allow the flavor to escape, keeping intact so it does not fall apart in the simmering curry or soup.

Minced to be used as is: Carefully cut the trimmed stalk in half lengthwise, then cut off the hard core at the bottom. Next cut each half lengthwise into fine long strips. Turn these 90 degrees and cut perpendicularly (⅛ inch/3 mm maximum) to create a fine mince of lemongrass. Then cut back and forth a few times to make sure it is all cut evenly.

Bruised for Infusion

Use a blunt object to bruise the stalk.

Thinly sliced for garnish or paste

1 Cut the trimmed stalk in half lengthwise.

2 Cut very thinly into crescent-shaped slices.

Making a Thai Spice Paste

Mortar and Pestle

Mortar and Pestle, Blender, or Food Processor

Candidly, it was only in the last few years I realized that using a mortar and pestle instead of a knife or even food processor can actually save you time. Really! Suppose you need some nuts to top a salad, a few swift swings of the pestle and a handful of nuts takes on a special crushed texture that grips onto every bite of shredded papaya tossed in a salty-spicy and only slightly sweet dressing (Green Papaya Salad Noodle Bowl, page 98). A quick rinse is all it takes to clean the stone mortar.

Take that same handful of nuts, pull out the cutting board, secure it on the counter, select a knife, start chopping trying to make sure they don't jump off the board as they are cut by the thin blade (it seems as if you sometimes chase them rolling around the board), then gather these up, clean the board. The resulting sharp edged peanuts but do not possess the same soulful misshaped texture that was created by pounding. Using a food processor requires minor set-up and major clean-up. This is one of many examples that using your hands will not only yield a better result, it will also be easier.

Chopping nuts is only one illustration, making a large spice paste is a whole different thing. Even though a hand pounded spice paste will last longer, and have a more desirable texture it will take you considerable more time to make. This book is based on the less laborious machine assisted spice pastes (store bought). If you cook often you may want to consider buying a spice paste grinder.

For a detailed step-by step videos with me showing you the technique for using a mortar and pestle visit (chefdanhi.com) or open up my first book *Southeast Asian Flavors* in the "Building Southeast Asian Flavors" chapter. Here I will focus on using electric machines.

So, yes, I do condone using a blender or food processor, yet there are some guidelines to follow to do this successfully.

Cutting Ingredients: Using your knife for a moment before making a paste will save you time struggling with the paste and give you the most consistent results.

• Thinly slicing fibrous ingredients like lemongrass, galangal, and ginger across the fibers is essential. Once they are added, any uncut fiber will simply turn into hair-like threads within the paste, hence the need to cut thinly first, then you can mince or grind these pieces.
• Roughly chop, slice, and crush garlic, shallots, chilies, and other aromatics. This encourages easier grinding, otherwise large pieces may bounce around and not get caught by the blade.
• Dry toast spices in a pan and cool, then pre-grind in a spice grinder. Whole spices will not grind properly in a blender.

Mortar and pestles allow you to pound only the ingredients you need.

Blenders are fast, however require adding liquid.

Food processors allow you to roughly large batches of chilies quick.

Equipment: Make sure to use a machine with a sharp blade, something most people overlook, if you have had it for many years and it's dull you may want to bring the blade to a knife sharpener for a touch up, it will make a difference with all of your blending.

• Blender: The advantage of a blender is that with a small area where the blade is located creates a vortex pulling all the ingredients to the bottom and they get puréed efficiently and evenly. The disadvantage is that you need to add a liquid to lubricate the mixture in order for it to grind. If oil will be used to fry the paste you can use that oil or small amounts of water can be used to facilitate blending. Two drawbacks to this—adding water increase the water activity that makes the paste very perishable, the flavor will deteriorate quickly in the refrigerator, maybe one week is okay, you must freeze it for longer storage. Secondarily, when you fry the paste the water prevents the ground aromatics to fry properly until the water has evaporated—making the cooking process

more lengthy and, debatably, changing the taste.

• Food Processor: A mini-food processor or full sized model can both be used. The disadvantage of a food processor is that the blades sit along the flat wide base, and opposite of a blender the ingredients tend to bounce around avoiding the whirling blades. Unless you have a significant amount it is also hard to get the ingredients to form a paste requiring stopping often to scrape down the sides.

• Wet Spice Paste Grinder: These powerful grinders work like a processor but with a built in spatula, designed to be inside the work bowl as it is running without hitting the running blades to force ingredients back onto cutting blades. This makes it possible to create a paste without adding water or oil, the same major benefit of a mortar and pestle. For really large batches I have seen excellent results with a meat grinder, beginning with a large die and progressively moving down to finer diameter dies.

Technique: All your ingredients are ready, you have the equipment selected, now it's time to create the aromatic spice paste. By now you may be considering buying the paste already prepared, right? For me it depends the mood I am in and how much time I have.

1 Prepare the ingredients as described above.
2 Begin by adding the wetter ingredients first (opposite of what you do with a mortar). Place the pre-cut shallots, garlic, and chilies in the chosen machine, pour in the oil that the paste will be fried in, if any. Purée these ingredients to create a wet paste, stopping to scrape down the sides as needed.
3 Then add the next set of dry ingredients, try to grind into a semi-smooth paste. Add small amounts of water only as necesssary to facilitate blending.

Making a Coconut Curry

A rainbow of colors can be found within the hundreds of curries around the different regions of Thailand. Some southern style curries are redolent of coconut milk, chili packed spice paste, and shrimp (Yellow Curry Shrimp, page 73). Take a trip to the northeast area of Issan and find jungle curries (Mixed Vegetable Jungle Curry, page 91) that are a highly spiced, vegetable packed broth absent of coconut milk. Since Thai coconut curries are the most popular around the world that is what I will focus on in this section. There are more than a half dozen curry recipes in the book, each recipe will also give you insight into the truly Thai style curries and if you want more information look at pages 158–169 of my first book, *Southeast Asian Flavors*.

Curry pastes, store-bought or homemade, lay the foundational flavor profile and closely create the categorical color of the curry. Curries are red from dried and fresh chilies, green from coriander and green chilies and yellow stained from the rhizome turmeric.

Making Thai curries is quite an easy cooking method, yes, in Thailand they traditionally use a brass wok-style pot but really all you need is a saucepan, a spoon or heat-proof spatula, and the chosen ingredients. Curries in Thailand are often made in large batches, brought to the market and left at room temperature and dished out as ordered. This being the case, you should not hesitate to make curries ahead and reheat when you are ready to eat—either later the same day or even later that week (sometimes I reserve delicate vegetables or herbs to add when I reheat the curry). They don't freeze well, usually coconut based curries separate after being defrosted.

To presume I can summarize all Thai curries into this small section is almost insulting to thousands of years of evolution, what I am trying to do here instead of an all encompassing summary is to give you a place to start. Here is a guideline of how much to use of each major component.

BASIC COCONUT CURRY FORMULA
1²/₃ cups (400 ml) coconut milk (1 can)
¼ cup (65 ml) curry paste
1 cup (250 ml) mild stock—chicken, pork, seafood, or vegetable
2–3 cups of bite-sized pieces of vegetables
Seasonings: 2 tablespoons Thai palm sugar and 1 teaspoon fish sauce

SIMMERING AROMATICS (optional—but recommended with pre-made pastes)
A few stalks of bruised lemongrass (tender inner part of bottom third only), 6 kaffir lime leaves and or a few slices of galangal

FINISHING AROMATICS
½–1 cup (15–30 g) Thai basil leaves
¼ cup (10 g) coriander leaves (cilantro)
1 tablespoon thinly sliced kaffir lime leaves

GARNISHES
Fresh herbs such as coriander leaves (cilantro) scattered around
A few spoonfuls of coconut milk drizzled on top
Table salad of cabbage, cucumbers, or long beans to snack on between bites
Condiments like chopped chilies, pickled mustard greens or lime wedges used to accent the curry the way you like

Each ingredient above is included in the chapter "Stocking Your Thai Panty," so look there for details on origins, flavors, appearance, shopping tips, and even substitutions.

LET'S MAKE A THAI CURRY—STEP-BY-STEP

1 Heat ½ cup (125 ml) of the coconut milk in a small saucepan over medium-high heat, cook, stirring constantly, until it reduces by about half and thickens considerably and begins to separate (about 5 minutes). This important step is called "cracking the coconut milk."
2 Mix in the curry paste and cook for an additional minute.

3 Pour in the remaining coconut milk, stock, simmering aromatics, protein, and vegetables and bring to a boil. Lower the heat to simmer for 3–5 minutes, until the protein and vegetables are cooked. Sometimes I add vegetables in stages to cook them each as desired.
4 Taste the sauce and adjust seasoning with fish sauce, salt and/or sugar.

5 Stir in the finishing aromatics, remove from the heat and spoon into a bowl
6 Garnish with desired items and serve with condiments and steamed rice.

Stir-frying 101

What is stir-frying, really? Stir-frying at home is not like stir-frying over a roaring fire in a restaurant. Their wok burner emits about 120,000 BTU (British Thermal Units) of heat while a home cooktop averages 10,000 BTU. To achieve the best results I deconstructed the methods and re-assembled them to get the desirable results. If you want to buy an relatively inexpensive wok burner get a "turkey fryer" burner for under US$100 and you are all set. Asian restaurant suppliers usually have single propane charged burners for under US$75, and most high end home stove manufacturers are now producing wok burners with higher BTU than the rest of the burners. I bought a professional wok burner, converted to propane for mobility and I have a professional powered burner for around US$900, worth every penny for a wok-aholic like myself.

I can only dedicate a small synopsis to the complex art of stir-frying. Grab a copy of *Breath of a Wok* or her more recent *Stir-frying To The Sky's Edge* by Grace Young to begin to understand the nuances to preparation, equipment selection and the complete cooking process to achieve the illusive *wok hei* flavor. I also wrote an article for *Fine Cooking* magazine back in 2003—"Stir-frying without Recipes," which is posted on their website. *Wok hei* is translated as breath of the wok, as the intense heat vaporizes fats, browns meats and caramelizes the vegetables natural sugars this subtle flavor is conjured up. This flavor does not last for long, try tasting your creation 10 minutes later and it will diminish noticeably.

To get ready to stir-fry, get organized! Read the recipe a couple of times (and have it at the ready for quick reference), line up all the prepared vegetables, marinated meat or seafood, sauces in the order that they will go in the pan. It's is best to even combine ingredients in stages—if onions and Chinese broccoli go in at the same time—combine them ahead of time. If the fish sauce, oyster sauce, and sugar go in together, whisk them in a small bowl first. These steps allow you to add items quickly, delays can cause garlic to burn, meat to toughen and veggies to become limp! Also have your bowl, plate or platter ready for the finished dish!

Getting to know fundamental ratios that work in the kitchen enable you to adapt more easily, learn the technique, and focus less on the recipe.

1–2 tablespoons oil
¾–1 lb (350–500 g) of prepared protein
Aromatics as needed
3–5 cups, about ¾–1 lb (350–500 g) prepared vegetables
¼–1 cup (65–250 ml) sauce

Oil with a high smoking point is best—the most common ones, listed from highest to lowest smoke points, are: safflower, cottonseed, grape seed, canola, soy, and peanut.

Marinating the meat or seafood will help ensure tenderness and moistness. First slice into bite-sized strips or slices, cut against the grain of the meat for maximum tenderness. I find the simplest one ingredient marinade is oyster sauce (or substitute vegetarian stir-fry sauce). Originally the Chinese developed a technique called velveting, where marinating in a mixture of rice wine, soy sauce, egg whites, cornstarch, and salt is used then a delicate pre-cooking in heated oil, 280°F (140°C), or some have turned to simmering water to reduce the fat content. These are added to the wok for a brief stir-frying to complete cooking, combine with other ingredients and coat with sauce.

Minced ginger, garlic, and green onions (scallions) are considered the holy trinity of Chinese stir-fries since many begin with these, in Thailand it is not as universal and ingredients like minced chilies, lemongrass, galangal, coriander (cilantro) root, and other spices may be included. Similar to the Mixed Vegetable Jungle Curry (page 91), the type of veggies added are up to you, how you cut them and when you add them may take some thought. I break vegetables into three categories—long, quick, and instant cooking. You can add these in stages or cut the longer cooking vegetable smaller (or blanch them ahead) so they cook at the same rate. This takes a bit of experimenting so have fun practicing.

- **Long Cooking:** Eggplant, long beans, onions, carrots
- **Quick Cooking:** Mushrooms, chilies, peppers, beans, asparagus, green papaya
- **Instant Cooking:** Asian greens (choy sum, bok choy…), snow peas, cooked bamboo shoots

Thais use far less cornstarch thickened sauces than the Chinese and most of their stir-fries have a smaller amount of sauce. Spice pastes, chili sauces, and a combination of a few ingredients like oyster sauce, soy sauce, and fish sauce is usually all it takes.

Step-by Step Stir-frying Success: Using ¾ lb (350 g) meat, most burners can handle this stir-fry in one go, if in doubt, cook the protein until 50% cooked, remove and reserve then cook your vegetables and aromatics and add the meat back in when they are cooked for a quick toss in the sauce.

1 Heat a large skillet, 10–14 inches (25–35 cm) or wok over high heat. If you have an electric burner use a flat bottomed wok. Swirl the oil in the skillet to coat the entire surface, and keep heating the skillet until it is very hot and the oil begins to smoke.
2 Stir-fry the marinated protein until 50% cooked, about 1–2 minutes.
3 Add the aromatics and vegetables and stir-fry for 1–3 minutes, then add the sauce mixture. Cook until the protein and vegetables are coated and cooked through.
4 Stir in the fresh herbs such as basil leaves and remove from the heat.
5 Taste and adjust seasoning as desired.
6 Spoon onto a serving platter and garnish as desired.

Coal is still used in homes, restaurants and on the streets of Thailand. I quickly grab this photo before the cook fired up our noodle dinner.

Planning a Thai Menu

Planning that perfect menu requires evaluating many factors—the occasion, day of the week, time of day, the flavors of each dish, the balance among dishes, where and when each item will be cooked, what is in season and what equipment is used. Here are a few suggested menus with guidelines on what can be done ahead of time.

Cook Ahead Weeknight Meal: All of these dishes can be prepared ahead of time and reheated, if necessary, for dinner. It's great for leftovers, so make double.

Thai Iced Tea (page 114)
• Make up to 3 days ahead: Make the tea base.
• That night: Crush ice, fill glasses, top with tea and finish with either water and lime or evaporated milk.

Five Spice Slow-cooked Pork (page 66)
• Make it up to 5 days ahead: cool and refrigerate.
• That night: Slowly heat up in a saucepan or microwave.

Asian Greens with Roasted Garlic (page 87)
• Make up to 2 days ahead. Clean the greens, spin them dry and prep all other ingredients.
• That night: A quick stir-fry is all it takes.

Jasmine Rice (page 102)
• Make up to 2 days ahead: Cook in rice cooker (or pan on the day you're serving it).
• That night: Warm in steamer or microwave.

Coconut Pudding with Seasonal Fruit (page 111)
• Make up to 3 days ahead: Prepare pudding and chill.
• That night: Dice fruit and spoon on puddings.

Drink Pairing
• Medium Bodied Red Wine.

Friday Night Cocktail Party: Some old and new friends are coming, it's a night to impress with your new Thai recipes. The work week limits prep time so some dishes can be pre-made.

Coconut Crusted Peanuts (page 43)
• Make up to 1 week ahead, and store in an air-tight container.

Grilled Chicken Wings with Tangy Chili Glaze (page 46)
• Marinate wings one or two days ahead.
• Grill wings one day before and refrigerate to re-heat in the oven on Friday. Otherwise, grill them before the party begins and keep them warm in the oven.

Golden Pork Satays with Thai Peanut Dip (page 40)
• Marinate pork Thursday, cook on Friday evening.
• Make sauce on Wednesday, reheat on Friday evening.

Citrus Salad with Crispy Shallots (page 54)
• Whisk all of the liquid ingredients together on Thursday.
• Cut fruit and vegetables, keeping each ingredient separate until just before the party. Then combine all the ingredients before guests arrive and serve.

Spiced Mango Cocktail (page 113)
• Purée can be made and held days ahead of time and then combined with ginger ale and garnish when ready to serve.

Other Drink Pairings:
• A bucket filled with ice, Thai beers, and sparkling wines.
• Lemongrass Iced Tea (page 115) with addition of vodka, mint, and soda water.
• Hot Thai Coffee (page 114) is sure to wake them up when they find themselves needing a recharge to keep partying all night long. Set the coffee maker up before they arrive or make the stove-top method and reheat when needed.

Weekend Afternoon in the Kitchen: Some weekends are meant to be spent cooking with friends and family. This menu gives everyone something to do while you hang out and have fun.

Snack On These As They Are Ready
• Thai Spring Rolls (page 44)
• Red Curry Shrimp Cakes (page 48)

Sit down for a Break
• Marinated Cucumber, Ginger and Thai Basil (page 58)
• Fire-roasted Shrimp (page 74)
• Mixed Vegetable Jungle Curry (page 91)
• Coriander Beef (page 69)
• Rice Ribbon Noodles with Basil (page 96)

Sip All Day Long
• Lemongrass Iced Tea (page 115)
• Iced Bottles of Sparkling Wine and Beer

Invite a Date Night
Spiced Mango Cocktail (page 113)
• Make up to 2 days ahead: Prepare mango purée, but don't add the ginger ale.
• That day: Cut the limes, cut the chilies, pick the basil.

• Time to cheers: Show off your mixoligist talents (that you rehearsed) as you assemble drink. Add ginger ale to mango. Fill the glasses with ice, pour in the mango mixture, playfully squeeze the lime, carefully garnish with chiles (those hands can cause pain later), push in the basil sprig and make a toast.

Silky Butternut Squash Coconut Soup (page 52)
• Make up to 1 day ahead: Cut all vegetables. Prepare all aromatics and herbs.
• That day: Make soup base (step 1), chill.
• Before you sit down to eat: Bring your date into the kitchen as you make the final touches for that special meal. Guide them (let the recipe in this book help) to make the soup as you whip up the stir-fry. Heat up soup, squash, coconut milk, then green onions (scallions). Stir in the basil.

Tamarind Soy Chicken with Cashews (page 63)
• Make up to 2 days ahead: Marinate the chicken.
• Make up to 1 day ahead: Cut the vegetables. Roast the cashews.
• That day: Measure out tamarind and soy sauce. Clean the basil. Get your stir-fry equipment and area organized.
• Before you sit down to eat: Pre-heat that wok and discuss the nuances of stir-frying (see page 30) as you follow steps 3–6 on the recipe.

Fresh Mangos in Sweet Coconut Cream with Roasted Peanuts (page 112)
• Make up to 2 days ahead: Make the coconut cream.
• That day: Peel and dice the fruit.
• Before you sit down to eat: Simply spoon on the fruit and smile, the rest of the night is time to relax and enjoy.

Basic Recipes

Dazzling red chili sauces and shatteringly crisp golden brown shallots are common garnishes for the foods of Thailand. Paying attention to these seemingly small accents can transform a good dish into a great culinary experience. Don't fret though, you don't have to make everything from scratch; in reality, most home cooks in Thailand buy premade curry pastes, chili pastes, and other kitchen essentials. Even though these might not be homemade it doesn't prevent these home cooks from creating amazing flavors and textures.

If you are going to purchase these items make sure to look at the "Stocking Your Thai Pantry" chapter (page 12) for tips on what to look for on the label, which brand I recommend, and how to store them to preserve their quality. Go to chefdanhi.com for the most up-to-date listing. Yet, there will be times when you may want to delve deeper and make a few of these foundational elements from scratch. For those of you that live in areas that don't have well-stocked Asian markets I've provided some simple basic recipes that will enable you to cook most of the dishes in the book. Don't be afraid to make large batches because most store in the refrigerator, but if you make a really large batch freezing is also okay.

One of my favorite recipes is the Thai Chili Jam (page 36), it is one of the most versatile ingredients in the Thai kitchen. Soups, sauces, and salad dressings in this book will use it as a foundation, but don't forget to be creative, it can be as simple as slathering this chili jam on some bread, layering some thin wafers of cucumber on top for a quick sandwich or even adding a spoonful to some of your old standby recipes to give it that Thai twist of *umami* and chili essence. If you are looking for a bolder, spicier condiment, try making your own Sriracha Chili Sauce (page 35).

With these building blocks of flavor on hand, I'm sure you will find yourself sprinkling fried garlic on many salads, pouring a little bit of that Thai Sweet Chili Sauce in your next barbecue marinade, or even adding a bit of that tart tamarind pulp to a Friday night cocktail… Go ahead and get creative! Buy it or make it? Throughout the book I have provided you with options to make most things from scratch or give you the information needed to buy the best items all ready to go. Stocking Your Own Thai Pantry chapter will be the most help here.

Fried Chilies

These fiery deep roasted chilies are used in Thailand in countless ways, tossing them in right before serving a hot and sour soup is a sure way to heat up the broth, used as a garnish for salads or tossed with snacking peanuts allows those that like it spicy to nibble on them, others can simple avoid biting down on them.

Makes ¼ cup (10 g)   Preparation time: 1 min
Cooking time: 5 mins

½ cup (125 ml) oil
¼ cup (6 g) dried red finger-length chilies

1 Heat the oil in a small skillet, saucepan, or wok until it is 350ºF (175ºC).
2 Add the chilies to the hot oil and fry for just a few seconds, until they lighten in color and become crispy (about 5 seconds).
3 Quickly remove the chilies and allow to drain and cool on a plate lined with a few layers of paper towels. They only keep for about a week, after which they start to age quickly.

Sriracha Chili Sauce Nahm Prik Sriracha

Recently acquiring culinary celebrity status, originating in a small seaside town in the gulf of Thailand, once simply a table condiment, this chili sauce is now used as a major seasoning. This chili sauce has become a favorite with Asian and Western cooks alike. You can buy the bottled sauce on your grocer's shelf or make this simple version. The traditional version is fermented before it is cooked, giving the sauce a deeper flavor.

Makes 1½ cups (375 ml)   Preparation time: 5 mins   Cooking time: 10 mins

¾ lb (350 g) red finger-length chilies, roughly chopped
4–6 cloves garlic, roughly chopped
½ teaspoon sea salt or kosher salt
1 tablespoon fish sauce (optional)
1 tablespoon sugar
1 cup (250 ml) water
¼ cup (65 ml) distilled white vinegar

1 Combine the chilies, garlic, salt, fish sauce, sugar, and water in a small saucepan and bring to a boil. Lower the heat, simmer for 3 minutes. Remove from the heat and cool to room temperature.
2 Transfer the boiled ingredients to a blender, add the vinegar and purée until very smooth, about 2 minutes.
3 Strain through a fine wire mesh strainer. Taste and adjust seasoning with vinegar, sugar, and salt.
4 Store in the refrigerator for up to a month or two.

Thai Sweet Chili Sauce Nahm Jim Gai

This thick, sweet, savory, sour, and spicy sauce has become one of my favorites, always on hand as a dip for vegetables or spring rolls. I like to use it as a base for a sauce, or for basting when I am grilling meat or fish. Traditionally, this sauce was used in the Northeast of Thailand for grilled chicken, similar to the Grilled Lemongrass Chicken (page 64). It only takes a few moments to use the mortar and pestle for grinding the chilies and garlic, actually faster than mincing by hand and I like the jagged edges that you will see floating in the transparent sauce.

Makes 1 cup (250 ml)   Preparation time: 5 mins   Cooking time: 10 mins

2 tablespoons minced or pounded red finger-length chilies
1 Thai chili, minced or pounded
1 tablespoon minced or pounded garlic
1½ teaspoons sea salt or kosher salt
1¼ cups (300 g) sugar
2 tablespoons fish sauce
¾ cup (180 ml) distilled white vinegar
½ cup (125 ml) water

1 Combine all the ingredients in a small saucepan and bring to a boil. Boil over medium heat for 10 minutes or until the mixture has reduced to 1 cup (250 ml). It will thicken further as it cools.
2 Remove from the heat and cool to room temperature before storing in the refrigerator for up to a few months.

Thai Chili Jam   Nahm Prik Pow

Jam-like in consistency, savory and sweet in taste, this multi-purpose sauce is used as a shortcut to flavor in today's Thai kitchens. Need to whip up a quick *tom yum*-like Hot and Sour Tamarind Soup (page 56), a few spoons of this will do it. if you want to add a rich flavor and reddish hue to fried rice, then you are also covered. Making your own Thai chili jam is worth the investment, make a large batch as it lasts for months in your refrigerator. When you buy the small dried shrimp, store them in the freezer to extend their shelf-life to nearly a year. However, if you're not interested in making your own, there are a few really good quality brands on the store shelves (go to chefdanhi.com for an updated list), labeled as Chili Paste in Soya Bean Oil.

Makes 1 cup (250 ml)   **Preparation time: 5 mins + soaking time + cooling time**   **Cooking time: 10 mins**

1 tablespoon dried shrimp
½ cup (125 ml) oil
1 cup (100 g) sliced shallots
½ cup (70 g) sliced garlic
¼ cup (6 g) dried red finger-length chilies
2 tablespoons fish sauce
2 tablespoons Tamarind Pulp or concentrate (page 25)
3 tablespoons Thai palm sugar or light brown sugar

1 Soak the shrimp in warm water for 5 minutes then drain and dry with paper towels. If you want to tame the heat of the chilies, remove the seeds.
2 Heat the oil in a large skillet or wok over medium heat; add the shrimp and cook until they darken, about 1 minute. Scoop out the shrimp and reserve. Fry the shallots in the same oil, stirring often until the edges are golden brown, about 2–4 minutes. Strain and reserve the shallots. Repeat with the garlic. Fry the chilies in the same oil until light in color, this is quick—about 5 seconds, set aside to cool.
3 Use a mini food processor or mortar to pulverize or purée the fried shrimp, shallots, garlic, and chilies until very fine or smooth. If using a processor you may need to use some of the frying oil to facilitate the puréeing.
4 Combine the purée with the remaining ingredients in a small saucepan or wok and boil for 1 minute stirring constantly. Remove from the heat and cool to room temperature, store in the refrigerator for up to 3 months.

Dried Shrimp: Small shrimp are salted and sun-dried to create a bright orange, salty-sweet ingredient essential to cuisines in this region. Every Southeast Asian country uses dried shrimp in its own way. In Thailand they are pounded and then used in salads such as the Thai green papaya salad (*som tom*). In Vietnam they're used to top small rice cakes with crispy pork and dried shrimp (*banh beo*), and in Malaysia they're used to enhance the broth of Malaysian coconut and lemongrass curry laksa. Although they possess a heady seafood aroma, these chewy seafood treasures can be addictive, so much so that I snack on them when using them in recipes. Look for bright orange, supple specimens. They are pounded into pastes, thrown raw into salads, and infused into broths.

Fried Shallots

Caramelized shallots are a universal garnish in Southeast Asia. Across the region home cooks, street food vendors, and fine dining restaurants alike use them. I often place them on the table during meal times and allow my friends and family to use them at will, adding crunch, sweet-n-bitter flavor notes to noodle soups, piles of rice or chilled salads. I usually buy mine in Malaysia and bring them back to keep in my freezer. When buying them pre-made here in the US, I look for those that list only shallots and oil in the ingredient list.

Makes about ½ cup (50 g)   **Preparation time: 5 mins + drying time**
Cooking time: 20 mins

6 shallots
½ cup (125 ml) oil

1 Trim off the root end of the shallots, then cut them in half lengthwise, peel and slice into even thin slices.
2 Air dry the sliced shallots on towel-lined baking sheet for 2 hours.
3 Combine the shallots and oil in a small skillet or wok over medium-low heat, stirring often until the shallots begin to sizzle. Lower the heat and continue to fry, stirring occasionally until the shallots turn light golden brown (about 15–20 minutes). Watch closely—the difference between golden and burnt is a matter of seconds.
4 When the shallots reach golden brown color, remove them with a heat-proof strainer, then spread them out on a few layers of paper towels.
5 Cool to room temperature before transferring to an air-tight container for storage.

Fried Garlic

I always keep a jar of these in my refrigerator using them to sprinkle on top of fried rice, in a bowl of noodle soup, or even to wake up some leftovers I brought back from a restaurant. I must admit I usually buy them already fried at the store in a small bag or jar. Either way they are a sure bet to add a depth of flavor and a bit of crunch.

Makes ½ cup (60 g)   **Preparation time: 5 mins + drying time**
Cooking time: 15 mins

10 cloves garlic
¼ cup (65 ml) oil

1 First decide how you want to cut the garlic. You can either chop it or make thin even slices, simply personal preference. Either way, try to make them as evenly cut as possible so they fry at the same rate.
2 Air dry the sliced or chopped garlic on a towel-lined baking sheet for 1 hour.
3 Combine the garlic and oil in a small skillet or wok over medium-low heat, stirring often until the garlic begins to sizzle. Lower the heat and continue to fry, stirring occasionally until light golden brown (about 15 minutes). Watch closely—the difference between golden and burnt is a matter of seconds.
4 When the garlic reaches golden brown color, remove them with a heat-proof strainer, then spread them out on a few layers of paper towels.
5 Cool to room temperature before transferring to an air-tight container. Best if stored in the refrigerator for a couple of weeks, or in the freezer for a few months.

Chapter One

Snacks and Appetizers

Thai people eat all day long and so do I. Instead of a few large meals, I create the opportunity to experience assorted flavors throughout the day. As a rule there is no time of day that food isn't available in Thailand, which is one of my favorite things about Southeast Asia!

The almost daunting variety of snacks available at a typical market can overwhelm even the most seasoned traveler. This is one reason I like to travel with a large group of people: we can buy more items and try more things. Yet, when I do hit the road alone, I still don't hold back and buy way more samples than I could ever eat by myself. Often I'll find myself sharing my edible discoveries with locals and fellow travelers…it's a great way to make friends. It's kind of funny, sometimes it turns into a exchange program, I offer some Coconut Crusted Peanuts (page 43) and they offer a cool beer in return—the Thais are very generous and kind.

Try the recipes in this chapter as mid-day snacks, light lunches, casual weekday meals, or part of an elegant cocktail party. You can always plan ahead, the sauces will keep well in the refrigerator or can even be frozen, you can marinate the meat, pickle the vegetables—a lot of these things can be done ahead of time.

The Grilled Chicken Wings with Tangy Chili Glaze (page 46) will make you wonder why chicken wings are not grilled more often. Of course, they taste best right off the grill, but I have grilled large batches (by tripling or quadrupling the ingredients), sealed them tight, and froze them. Then making some small packs of sauce, then giving them to friends and family to heat up in the oven, toss in sauce for a taste of Thailand.

Coconut Crusted Peanuts (page 43) can be made ahead of time and can be at the ready for any moment you want a snack or an unexpected guest shows up, or you're invited to a party where everyone brings a taste of something special—I guarantee they're always a hit. I've even used them as a garnish sprinkled on top of a salad or stir-fry. All of these recipes are great served as they are, but don't be afraid to experiment and try some new ways to serve them.

Golden Pork Satays with Thai Peanut Dip

Slender slivers of grilled curry marinated pork are always a favorite at parties. If you don't have the time to skewer the meat, use the same marinade on pork chops or even chicken thighs and simply grill the larger pieces over a lower heat. I always pan-roast or deep-fry the peanuts myself for the deepest flavor possible (see page 24), if you must, you can oven roast or buy them already roasted (unsalted and unseasoned—read that label). Don't use peanut butter unless you see it ground in front of you solely from peanuts, most shelved brands add ingredients that change the flavor profile of the finished sauce completely.

Makes about 30 skewers
Preparation time: 10 mins + marinating time
Cooking time: 20 mins

30 bamboo skewers, about 6 inches
   (15 cm) in length
1½ lb (750 g) pork leg, shoulder (butt), or
   loin
2 tablespoons yellow curry paste
¼ teaspoon turmeric powder
¼ cup (75 g) Thai palm sugar or light
   brown sugar
1 tablespoon fish sauce
2 tablespoons coconut milk

THAI PEANUT DIP
1½ cups (400 ml) coconut milk
2 tablespoons red curry paste
¼ teaspoon turmeric powder
½ cup (125 ml) water
3 tablespoons Thai palm sugar or light
   brown sugar
1 tablespoon fish sauce
6 kaffir lime leaves (substitute 1 teaspoon
   finely grated lime zest)
½ cup (75 g) roasted or deep-fried peanuts

1 Pour some boiling water on top of the skewers, let them cool to room temperature. This helps keep the meat from sticking and makes them resist burning.
2 Cut the pork into flat strips, about 3 x ¾ inch and ⅛ inch thick (7.5 cm x 2 cm x 3 mm). Whisk together the curry paste, turmeric powder, sugar, fish sauce, and coconut milk together in a medium bowl to create a smooth paste. Add the sliced pork and gently massage so that every surface of the pork is coated. Marinate the pork for at least 30 minutes, ideally overnight.
3 Make the Thai Peanut Dip by heating ½ cup of the coconut milk in a small saucepan over medium-high heat, cook, stirring constantly, until it reduces by about half and thickens considerably (about 5 minutes). Mix in the curry paste and cook for an additional minute. Pour in the remaining coconut milk, turmeric powder, water, sugar, fish sauce, kaffir lime leaves and bring to a boil. Lower the heat to simmer for 2 minutes. Transfer to a blender, add the peanuts and carefully pureé until smooth. Taste and adjust seasoning with sugar, fish sauce and salt. Serve warm, room temperature, or chill for later use—it will thicken when cold, adjust with water/coconut milk if necessary.
4 Skewer the pork strips onto the bamboo skewers. Straighten the strips out so that it will cook evenly. Ideally use a charcoal grill to grill the satay, second choice is a gas grill, lastly you could use a stove-top grill pan. First, preheat the grill on high. Then, place a strip of foil parallel to the hottest part of the grill. Use this foil to protect the skewers from burning, and turn the skewers occasionally. Cook until the pork is golden brown (even dark brown in some areas) and cooked through, about 5–8 minutes. Serve with a dipping bowl of the Thai Peanut Dip on the side.

Right: Each trip to Thailand I wander the streets in search of tasty bites like these satay I found charring to perfection in the sleepy town of Lam Nari.

Crunchy Sweet Papaya Pickles

Sweet, sour, and salty pickles adorn tables across Thailand, sometimes eaten with the standard dishes of Thailand. I have taken the liberty of enriching the basic dressing with some red curry paste—a wallop of flavor in one spoonful. I have made these pickles with many fruits and vegetables, I recommend sticking with one or two varieties per batch. Try pickling carrots, cabbage, radish, firm honeydew, or cantaloupe, unripe mangos, or even pineapple. I find myself just snacking on these or you may want to serve them with these recipes: Coriander Beef (page 69); Bangkok "Night Market" Ramen (page 100); Roast Duck with Snow Peas and Mango (page 68); Garlic Crab with Green Beans (page 76); Garlic Soy Noodles with Pork (page 97); Cinnamon-scented Beef Noodle Soup (page 101), or Five Spice Slow-cooked Pork (page 66).

Serves 4–6
Preparation time: 5 mins
Cooking time: 10 mins

½ cup (125 ml) rice vinegar
½ cup (100 g) sugar
1 teaspoon sea salt or kosher salt
2 teaspoons red curry paste
1 tablespoon fish sauce
2 cups (250 g) unripe green papaya, cut into thin slices (see photo box below)

1 Whisk together the vinegar, sugar, salt, curry paste and fish sauce in a small saucepan. Bring to a boil and shut off immediately. Remove from the heat, cool to room temperature.
2 Pour over the papaya, pressing under the brine—it's okay if a few stick out of the top, the papaya will release some water and the next day they will be under the brine.
3 The next day, after giving them a stir—you can eat them right away or slowly tap into this storehouse of flavor over the next few weeks.

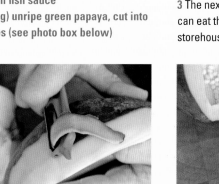

1 Peel the skin off the green papaya.

2 Cut the green papaya into bite-sized slices.

3 Pour the pickling liquid over the papaya.

Coconut Crusted Peanuts

Thais love to snack. When I am there the one snack that I am always on the look out for are oven-roasted fried peanuts, dried chilies, and kaffir lime leaves tossed in a tamarind glaze. The result is a sweet-sour-spicy flavor that never gets old. This recipe is inspired by this wonderful snack. Quality peanuts are essential, I prefer to buy raw peanuts and slowly roast them in a pan over low heat, tossing often—this takes about 15 minutes and the resulting semi-charred peanuts are fabulously flavored, or deep-fry them for a few minutes for a deep-roasted flavor. However, you may opt to buy dry roasted peanuts instead or even substitute cashews.

Serves 4–6
Preparation time: 5 mins
Cooking time: 15 mins

1¾ cups (250 g) roasted peanuts
2 tablespoons Thai sweet chili sauce
2 teaspoons sugar
½ teaspoon sea salt or kosher salt
1 stalk lemongrass, tender inner part of bottom third only, finely minced
1 teaspoon minced kaffir lime leaves (substitute 2 teaspoon lime zest)
½ teaspoon dried red chili flakes or ground dried red finger-length chilies
½ cup (40 g) dried unsweetened shredded or grated coconut

1 Toss the peanuts in a bowl with the chili sauce, sugar, salt, lemongrass, kaffir lime leaves, and chilies until coated evenly. Then add the coconut and toss again until it is evenly coated.
2 Spread them out on a non-stick baking mat or oiled baking sheet.
3 Bake in an oven preheated to 350°F (175°C) for 10–15 minutes or until the coconut is a golden brown.
4 Remove from the oven and let them cool before removing from the pan.

5 Keep the pan tightly covered until you're ready to serve—the peanuts tend to absorb humidity in the air. They last for a few weeks, the few days after they are made they are at their peak of flavor, the flavors have blended well yet they are still very crunchy.

Thai Spring Rolls

Making your own spring rolls is not as difficult as you think and it enables you to fill them with what you want. The Thai style spring roll differs from the Chinese version in that is has more ground meat and resilient bean thread noodles for a different textural experience. Thin flaky layers of spring roll skin succumb to each bite as you chomp down on rich mushrooms, and ground meat with sweet shavings of carrots.

Makes 10–12 rolls
Preparation time: 10 mins + assembling time
Cooking time: 5 mins

2 oz (60 g) dried bean thread noodles (cellophane noodles)
2 tablespoons oil (divided use)
1 tablespoon minced garlic
4 Thai chilies, minced
½ lb (250 g) ground chicken
1 cup (40 g) sliced fresh shiitake mushrooms (stems removed)
1 cup (75 g) shaved green cabbage
½ cup (70 g) shredded carrots
2 tablespoons soy sauce
1 tablespoon fish sauce
¼ teaspoon sea salt or kosher salt
⅛ teaspoon ground white pepper
2 tablespoons chopped coriander leaves (cilantro)
10–12 defrosted spring roll wrappers
1 large egg, beaten until smooth
Oil, for deep-frying

1 Pour some boiling water over the noodles, let soak for 5 minutes, drain and rinse with cool water. Cut the noodles so they are easier to roll (just snip a few times with a pair of scissors). Reserve at room temperature.

2 Heat a large skillet or wok over high heat. Swirl 1 tablespoon of the oil in the skillet to coat the entire surface, and keep heating the skillet until very hot and the oil begins to smoke. Add the garlic and chilies and stir-fry until aromatic but not brown, about 10 seconds. Add the chicken and continue to stir-fry breaking up the chicken until it is cooked, transfer to a bowl and reserve.

3 In the same skillet, add the remaining tablespoon of oil and heat over high heat. Add the mushrooms and stir fry until they wilt, add the cabbage, carrots, soy sauce, fish sauce, salt and white pepper, and cook until the cabbage wilts, about 3–5 minutes. Transfer the vegetable into a large mixing bowl, stir in the bean thread noodles, reserved chicken and coriander leaves. Let this mixture cool to room temperature. Squeeze out any excess moisture, a very important step!

4 Roll the spring rolls by peeling the layers of wrapper apart, re-stack them and keep them covered so they don't dry out. Place a wrapper on a clean work surface with the bottom corner facing you, place ¼ cup of the filling on the bottom third of the wrapper. Use your hand to form the filling into a cylinder shape, with 2 inch (5 cm) margin away from the left and right corners. Fold over the bottom corner and pull back to make taut. Roll over once, then fold in the side corners to form a tight seal, brush the top ⅓ of the wrapper with beaten egg, roll up to a tight cylinder. Fry immediately or refrigerate up to 8 hours or freeze for up to 3 months.

5 Deep-fry the spring rolls in preheated 350°F (175°C) oil for 3–5 minutes or until golden brown. Drain on paper towels. Serve with dipping sauces such as Thai Sweet Chili Sauce (page 35) or a mixture of soy sauce spiced up with chilies and tempered with sugar.

BBQ Corn with Sriracha

BBQ Corn with Sriracha

Koh Samui, the enchanted tropical island in the heart of Gulf of Thailand, is home to many gifted cooks. One street vendor showed me how simple grilled corn can be spiced up with a little Sriracha Chili Sauce. I tried to recreate this recipe and found that enriching the store-bought Sriracha chili sauce (or you can make your own by following the recipe on page 35) with aromatic lime-juice and coriander leaves (cilantro) made it taste even better. In Thailand, the corn is grilled without the husk, which allows the corn to scorch, creating a smoky flavor and chewy texture. Lightly brushing the corn with a mixture of oil, water, and fish sauce encourages the corn to steam while it is browning and seasons it at the same time.

Serves 4–6
Preparation time: 5 mins
Cooking time: 10 mins

6 ears of freshly husked corn
¼ cup (65 ml) water
3 tablespoons fish sauce
2 teaspoons oil

SRIRACHA SLATHER
½ cup (125 ml) Sriracha Chili
   Sauce (page 35)
1 tablespoon Thai palm
   sugar or light brown sugar
1 tablespoon fresh lime juice
1 teaspoon chopped coriander leaves (cilantro)

1 While the grill is preheating at its highest setting, remove the husks from the corn.
2 Whisk the water, fish sauce and oil together. Brush the corn with this mixture.
3 Make the Sriracha Slather by whisking together the Sriracha Chili Sauce, sugar, lime juice and coriander leaves. Pour into a serving bowl with a brush and set aside.
4 Grill the corn over high heat, basting occasionally with the fish sauce mixture until lightly browned in some places and the corn is cooked.
5 Serve with the bowl of Sriracha Slather and a brush.

Grilled Chicken Wings with Tangy Chili Glaze

Slowly grilling over indirect heat gives these wings a craveable crispy/chewy texture. Marinating them gives them a deep seasoning and then tossing in the aromatic kaffir lime leaf glaze creates an addictive flavor . . . you may want to double the recipe.

Serves 4–6
Preparation time: 10 mins + marinating time
Cooking time: 45 mins

12 chicken wings (about 2 lb/1 kg)
3 tablespoons fish sauce
1 tablespoon sugar
½ teaspoon ground white pepper
1 tablespoon oil

GLAZE
2 tablespoons chili paste in soya bean oil (*nahm prik pow*)
1 teaspoon minced kaffir lime leaves (substitute 2 teaspoons finely minced lime zest)
1 tablespoon fresh lime juice
1 tablespoon sugar
2 teaspoons minced ginger
1 tablespoon minced green onions (scallions)

1 Toss the chicken wings in the fish sauce, sugar, white pepper, and oil. Refrigerate and marinate for at least an hour, ideally overnight.
2 Preheat a charcoal or gas grill to medium heat. Grill the chicken wings over indirect heat for about 30–45 minutes turning them every 15 minutes until cooked through and golden brown.
3 Make the Glaze by whisking together all the ingredients in a large bowl. Toss the wings into the Glaze until well coated.

Sweet-n-Spicy Pork Ribs

Sweet-n-Spicy Pork Ribs

One bite of this sweet-n-spicy glaze coating these ribs and your taste buds will be captivated. Thai Sweet Chili Sauce (Nahm Jim Gai) (page 35) that is used for the glaze is traditionally used for grilled chicken in northeastern Thailand. Want an extra level of spice? Add minced chilies or ground dried red chilies, or increase the amount of Sriracha Sauce in the Chili Sauceto the marinade.

Serves 4–6
Preparation time: 10 mins + marinating time
Cooking time: 2 hours

6 lb (3 kg) pork ribs (baby back, spare, country, or St Louis style)
1 lime, cut into wedges

MARINADE
¼ cup (65 ml) fish sauce
¼ cup (65 ml) soy sauce
1 cup (300 g) Thai palm sugar or light brown sugar
2 teaspoons ground black pepper
2 tablespoons minced coriander stems (cilantro stems)

CHILI SAUCE
½ cup (125 ml) Thai Sweet Chili Sauce (page 35)
¼ cup (65 ml) Sriracha Chili Sauce (page 35)
¼ cup (65 ml) roughly chopped coriander leaves (cilantro)

1 First peel off the thin membrane on bone side or rib rack (this will toughen when cooked)
2 Make the Marinade by whisking together the fish sauce, soy sauce, sugar, black pepper, and coriander stems in a large bowl. Brush the ribs with the Marinade, transfer to a baking pan (meat side facing down), cover with plastic wrap and refrigerate for at least one hour, ideally overnight.
3 Preheat the oven to 350ºF (175ºC). Add ¼ cup (65 ml) of water to the baking pan with the ribs (meat side facing up), and tightly cover with aluminum foil. Bake for 1½ hours, remove from the oven and allow it to cool to room temperature drain any excess liquid, then use or store in the refrigerator for later use.
4 Preheat the grill or oven broiler until very hot.
5 Whisk together the ingredients for the Chili Sauce in a large bowl. Cut the ribs into individual ribs, and toss them into the Chili Sauce and save the sauce coated bowl. Grill or broil the ribs until they are brown, remove from the grill or broiler and toss back into the same bowl—using the sauce to give them a second coating and moist appearance. Arrange on a platter and serve with lime wedges.

Red Curry Shrimp Cakes

Using a food processor to make these shrimp cakes takes just a few minutes to prepare and the results are spectacular. These cakes can be served as a cocktail party appetizer, a snack at a casual weekend barbecue or even a weeknight dinner main dish. Chilling the shrimp in the freezer for 15 minutes before putting them in the blender ensures the springy texture of the cakes. I like serving these on a bed of lettuce leaves and fresh Thai herbs like coriander leaves (cilantro) and basil so that each person can make a lettuce wrap.

Makes 20 pieces
Preparation time: 7 mins + chilling time
Cooking time: 10 mins

8 oz (250 g) peeled and deveined raw
   shrimp, roughly chopped
2 tablespoons red curry paste
1 large egg
2 teaspoons fish sauce
1 tablespoon sugar
2 tablespoons coconut milk
¼ cup (25 g) chopped long beans or
   green beans
2 tablespoons roughly chopped Thai
   basil leaves
2 tablespoons oil

SWEET CILANTRO SAUCE
¼ cup (65 ml) Thai Sweet Chili
   Sauce (page 35)
1 tablespoon fresh lime juice
2 teaspoons chopped coriander
   leaves (cilantro)
1 teaspoon minced ginger

1 Prepare the Sweet Cilantro Sauce by whisking all the ingredients together in a small bowl and then set aside.

2 Spread the shrimp on a plate and chill the shrimp in the freezer for 15 minutes. Meanwhile get all your other ingredients ready. Combine the chilled shrimp, red curry paste, egg, fish sauce, sugar, and coconut milk in a food processor or blender. Process until smooth, about 30 seconds. Transfer the mixture to a mixing bowl. Mix in the green beans and basil.

3 Because different brands of curry pastes have differing amounts of salt you'll want to make a sample fish cake first. Sauté 1 tablespoon of the shrimp cake mixture in a skillet. Taste, and if necessary, adjust seasoning with fish sauce and salt.

4 Heat a large skillet over medium heat. First use 1 tablespoon of the oil to coat the skillet, use a measuring spoon to drop 1 tablespoon of the paste into the skillet. With a damp finger, flatten the paste slightly to about ½-inch/1.25-cm thick. Make about 10 of these shrimp patties in the skillet. Then cook the cakes until they are golden brown on each side and cooked through, about 2 minutes per side. Remove from the skillet and set aside. Wipe out the skillet with a paper towel, make more patties from the remaining paste and cook the same way. Serve with a side bowl of the Sweet Cilantro Sauce.

VARIATIONS
Fish Cakes—add one tablespoon of cornstarch.

Scallop Cakes—reduce the coconut milk by half, and add one tablespoon of cornstarch.

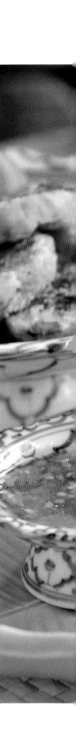

1 Spread the shrimp on a plate and chill in the freezer for 15 minutes.

2 Mix the green beans and basil with the shrimp mixture.

3 Flatten the paste slightly with a damp finger.

Chapter Two

Soups and Salads

Thailand's bounty of native produce empowers the cook to create a kaleidoscopic variety of salads. The very first time I went to Thailand two decades ago the universal and rhythmic pounding of the large wooden pestles that churn out papaya salad immediately captivated me, keeping me coming back year after year. Street food is king in Thailand, if you stop on almost any street corner and look around you're sure to find a few, if not dozens, makeshift food carts serving some of the most delicious street foods in the world. For about 40 Thai baht (about 1 US dollar) you can have a steaming bowl of soup filled with rice noodles, a side plate of herbs and bean sprouts to add crunch and aroma to every bite, this is food heaven!

Thailand could be crowned the champion of Southeast Asian salads. Begin your Thai salad journey with the Green Mango and Cashew Salad (page 57), its refreshingly bright and tart flavor is one that I never tire of, it wakes up my palate and reminds me why I have such a craving for the salads of Southeast Asia. Thai salads are not always comprised exclusively of vegetables or fruit, the Glass Noodle Salad (page 55) is a prime example, where resilient noodles make up the majority of the salad and strips of cucumber and bean sprouts add a cool crunch. Most Thai salads use lime juice to give them a pleasant acidity. The non-traditional Citrus Salad with Crispy Shallots (page 54) is one of those recipes where I took a classic dish called Yam Sam-O, and gave it a little twist with the addition of oranges—the combination of flavors makes something naturally delicious. The great thing about these salads is that they can be made ahead of time and brought to a party to show all your friends and family your new Thai cooking skills.

Soup is the ultimate global comfort food. Whether it be the classic, Hot and Sour Tamarind Soup (page 56), the Tart Orange Curry Soup (page 53), or the rich coconut laden favorites of the region, like the famed Chicken and Galangal Soup (Tom Kha Gai), which is a favorite around the world. Thai soups illustrate beautifully the universal truth that a "a bowl of soup can satisfy the soul." Speaking of creamy soups, make sure to try the Silky Butternut Squash Coconut Soup (page 52) with sweet wafers of pumpkin or butternut squash, an aromatic and slightly rich broth enriched with shiitake mushrooms and perfumed with anise-scented basil leaves.

Serves 4–6
Preparation time: 10 mins
Cooking time: 15 mins

3 tablespoons chili paste in soya bean oil
 (*nahm prik pow*)
2 tablespoons fish sauce
3 cups (750 ml) vegetable or chicken stock/
 broth
3¼ cups (800 ml) coconut milk (divided use)
3 stalks lemongrass, tender inner part of bottom
 third only, bruised
6 kaffir lime leaves (substitute 1 teaspoon finely
 grated lime zest)
6 slices galangal (substitute fresh ginger)
1 cup (40 g) fresh shiitake mushrooms, stems
 removed, cut into bite-sized halves or
 quarters
2 cups (225 g) kabocha squash (substitute but-
 ternut squash), ⅛ in (3 mm) thick bite-sized
 slices
½ cup (40 g) green onions (scallions), sliced
 into short lengths
¼ cup (7 g) Thai basil leaves, ripped into pieces

1 Whisk together the chili paste, fish sauce, chicken stock, and half of the coconut milk in a large saucepan. Drop in the lemongrass, kaffir lime leaves, galangal and mushrooms and heat these over a medium heat until simmering gently. Cook this for 5 minutes to ensure infusion of the flavors from the aromatics.
2 Stir in the *kabocha* squash and remaining coconut milk and simmer until just tender (be careful as the pumpkin seems firm for a few minutes then quickly gets very soft).
3 Stir in the green onions. Simmer for 1 more minute.
4 Remove from the heat, taste and adjust seasoning using fish sauce and/or salt. Stir in the basil leaves and serve immediately.

Silky Butternut Squash Coconut Soup

This coconut soup is rich yet light. Timidly sweet pumpkin slices are enveloped in a distinctly Thai aroma garnered from the stalks of lemongrass, kaffir lime leaves, and slices of galangal. These aromatics are used to infuse the broth and are left in as a garnish, make sure to tell your guest not to eat them. A handful of basil leaves gets stirred in at the very last moment with it's hint of anise.

Tart Orange Curry Soup

Serves 4–8
Preparation time: 10 mins
Cooking time: 10 mins

Tart orange curries are inherently simple to prepare and versatile in the ingredients you can use, including many types of seafood and vegetables. These central plains curries of Thailand are thinner than most others and don't use coconut milk, hence I felt they were a natural selection for transformation into a soup. David Thompson, the ultimate authority on Thai food, and hence culture, explains in his seminal book, *Thai Food*, that grilled fish is sometimes added. I know that a few flakes of charred fish or shrimp would be most welcome in this soup and adding some noodles would make it a complete meal.

2 tablespoons oil
5 tablespoons sour curry paste (substitute red curry paste)
½ teaspoon turmeric powder
4 cups (1 liter) chicken or seafood stock/broth
2 cups (500 ml) water
2 tablespoons sugar
1 cup (120 g) onions, bite-sized slices
1 cup (100 g) long beans or green beans, bite-sized pieces
1 cup (80 g) cabbage, bite-sized pieces
1 cup (150 g) bamboo shoots, bite-sized slices
1 cup (150 g) cherry or grape tomatoes, cut in halves or large diced tomatoes
3 tablespoons Tamarind Pulp or concentrate (page 25)
2 tablespoons fish sauce
2 tablespoons fresh lime juice
¼ cup (10 g) chopped coriander leaves (cilantro)
2 cups (80 g) watercress, sliced into small pieces (substitute choy sum, arugula or spinach)

1 Heat a large saucepan over medium-high heat, add the oil, curry paste, and turmeric. Stir while roasting the spices for 1 minute.
2 Mix in the stock, water, sugar, onions, beans, cabbage, bamboo shoots, and tomatoes. Bring to a boil for 3 minutes.
3 Stir in the tamarind, fish sauce, and fresh lime juice. Adjust the seasoning with fish sauce, salt, sugar, and tamarind.
4 Divide the chopped coriander leaves and watercress into the serving bowls. Ladle the hot soup into the bowls and serve.

Serves 4–6
Preparation time: 15 mins + chilling

2 cups (350 g) pomelo, peeled and crumbled, as shown below (substitute grapefruit)
2 oranges, peeled and deseeded, pulp torn into small pieces
1 lime, finely grated zest combined with juice
1 clove garlic, minced
1 shallot, thinly sliced
1–2 red finger-length chilies, thinly sliced
1 tablespoon fish sauce
1 teaspoon sugar
1 cup (20 g) mint leaves
2 cups (70 g) shredded green leaf lettuce, save some leaves for garnish
2 tablespoons Fried Shallots (page 37)

1 Gently fold the citrus, garlic, shallot, chilies, fish sauce, and sugar together in a medium bowl. Chill for ½ hour before serving, but no longer than 8 hours as the flavor begin to suffer.
2 Fold in the mint leaves, then taste and adjust seasoning with salt and sugar.
3 Put the lettuce leaves inside a shallow bowl, then spoon the citrus salad on top of the lettuce. Sprinkle with the Fried Shallots.

Citrus Salad with Crispy Shallots

The fragrant flavors reverberate on your tongue with this vibrant citrus salad. All citrus is believed to originate in Asia and this contemporary recipe shows how the flavors of Thailand can be applied to a newly founded fruit salad combination. Grilled or poached shrimp are a fantastic addition inside the salad, or use this as a base on a plate and top with a grilled fish, beef, pork, or chicken.

1 Cut the rind into equal segments by slicing it with a sharp knife. Be careful not to cut the inner segments.

2 Starting from the top of the cut, peel away the rind to expose the segments.

3 Remove the citrus membranes and separate the segments.

Glass Noodle Salad

Bright flavors, quick to prepare, and easy to make ahead, this side dish is a twist on Thai yam woon sen. The cooks of the small seaside town of Sriracha never dreamed that their own Nahm Prik Sriracha Chili Sauce (page 35) would be an international favorite, this recipe uses the brillant red sauce to add color and a spicy kick. Adding slices of grilled meats or seafood make it a more substantial meal, or keep it vegetarian by using soy sauce in place of the fish sauce.

Serves 4–6
Preparation time: 10 mins + marinating time

One 4 oz (120 g) packet or bundle of dried bean thread noodles (cellophane noodles)
¼ cup (40 g) thinly sliced red onions, soaked in ice water for 15 minutes, drained well
2 stalks lemongrass, tender inner part of bottom third only, finely minced
2 tablespoons fresh lime juice
2–3 tablespoons Sriracha Chili Sauce (page 35)
2 tablespoons fish sauce
1 tablespoon sugar
1 cup (125 g) matchstick strips cucumber
¼ cup (10 g) roughly chopped coriander leaves (cilantro)
1 cup (50 g) bean sprouts
¼ cup (5 g) mint leaves

1 Pour boiling water over the noodles and let soak for 5 minutes. Strain and rinse with water until cool, drain very well. Using scissors or knife, cut the noodles a few times to shorten the length, making them easier to eat. Transfer the noodles to a large mixing bowl.
2 Stir in the onions, lemongrass, lime juice, Sriracha Chili Sauce, fish sauce, sugar, cucumber, and coriander leaves. Make sure the noodles are thoroughly mixed with all the ingredients. Marinate in the refrigerator for at least 30 minutes or until ready to eat.
3 Fold in the bean sprouts and mint leaves. Adjust the taste by seasoning it with Sriracha, sugar, and, fish sauce.

Hot and Sour Tamarind Soup

Hot, sour, salty, sweet, and *umami* in every spoonful! This sensory experience is a great base recipe for you to make your own versions—add seafood like shrimp, scallops, and clams. If you can buy the shrimp with the heads on, then peel them, saving all the shells, and simmer the peeled shrimp with the broth for 10 minutes, then proceed with the recipe below—this will result in a deep shrimp flavor. Traditionally, lemongrass, kaffir lime leaves and galangal are left in most Thai soups, make sure to tell your guests to eat around the lime leaves or you can remove them before serving.

Serves 4–6   Preparation time: 10 mins
Cooking time: 15 mins

1 small package (about 2 oz/60 g) dried bean thread noodles (cellophane noodles)
6 tablespoons chili paste in soya bean oil (*nahm prik pow*)
8 cups (2 liters) chicken or seafood stock/broth
2 tablespoons fish sauce
8 slices galangal (substitute ginger)
4 stalks lemongrass, tender inner part of bottom third only, bruised
8 kaffir lime leaves (substitute 2 teaspoons finely grated lime zest)
4–6 Thai chilies, smashed
1 cup (150 g) cherry or grape tomatoes, cut in halves, or large diced tomatoes
1 can (15 oz/425 g or 7 oz/200 g drained weight) straw mushrooms, cut in halves
½ cup (125 ml) Tamarind Pulp or concentrate (page 25)
2 tablespoons fresh lime juice
¼ cup (7 g) Thai basil leaves
1 lime, cut into wedges

1 Pour boiling water over the noodles, let soak for 5 minutes, drain and rinse with cool water. Cut the noodles so they will fit on a soup spoon (just snip with a pair of scissors). Reserve at room temperature.
2 Combine the chili paste, stock, fish sauce, galangal, lemongrass, kaffir lime leaves and chilies in a large saucepan. Bring the mixture to a boil, lower the heat to simmer for 5 minutes.
3 Stir in the tomatoes and straw mushrooms and simmer for 2 minutes. Stir in the tamarind and lime juice.
4 Taste and adjust the seasoning with fish sauce, sugar, and tamarind.
5 Divide the noodles and basil leaves into serving bowls, ladle the soup over the basil leaves and serve immediately with lime wedges on the side.

Green Mango and Cashew Salad

Each bite is packed with explosions of tart, sweet, salty, and spicy shards of mango and roasted cashews with aromatic fresh lime juice. This Thai salad (*yum*) is a quintessential example of the Thai balance of tastes: *umami*-filled salty fish sauce, rich palm sugar, and sour mangos. If you can't get your hands on some unripe mangos, try some other fruits, such as green apples, unripe papaya, or even pineapple, but make sure to adjust your seasoning to match the fruit you select. Lately I have been adding pan-roasted shavings of fresh coconut to the salad.

Serves 4–6
Preparation time: 12 mins

2 cloves smashed garlic
8 thin slices ginger
2–4 Thai chilies
3 tablespoons fresh lime juice
1 tablespoon Thai palm sugar or light brown sugar
1 tablespoon fish sauce
Pinch of sea salt or kosher salt
¼ cup (25 g) thinly sliced shallots
2–3 large unripe mangos or 4-5 small mangos (about 4 lb/1.5 kg), peeled, seed removed and cut into matchstick strips to yield 6 cups (1.25 kg)
2 teaspoons finely sliced kaffir lime leaves (about 6 leaves) or 1 teaspoon minced lime zest
¼ cup (10 g) roughly chopped coriander leaves (cilantro)
¼ cup (40 g) crushed or chopped toasted cashews

1 Pound the garlic, ginger and chilies using a mortar and pestle, or pulse in a processor until it forms a coarse paste. Add the lime-juice, sugar, fish sauce, and salt. Mix until the sugar is dissolved. While massaging gently, rinse the shallots under cool running water for 15 seconds—this will reduce the raw flavor, set aside. Use this dressing to coat the shallots, mangos, kaffir lime leaves, and coriander leaves.
2 Take a big bite of the coated mango and adjust seasoning with lime juice, fish sauce, sugar, and salt.
3 Spoon onto serving bowl and sprinkle with the chopped cashews.

Marinated Cucumber, Ginger and Thai Basil

In Thailand, every time I order a grilled satay, it comes with the pickled cucumber or *achat*, and I am left wanting more. This easy to make tangy cucumber salad stands on its own as a side dish to a meal or I find it makes a wonderful complement to a grilled piece of fish, add some steamed rice and you'll have a light meal.

Serves 4–6
Preparation time: 10 mins + resting time

2 cups (250 g) cucumber strips, (the kirby variety preferred)
½ teaspoon sea salt or kosher salt
1 medium shallot, halved and thinly sliced
2 tablespoons rice vinegar (unseasoned)
2 tablespoons sugar
1 tablespoon fish sauce
1 tablespoon very thin strips of fresh ginger
1 red finger-length chili, thinly sliced
¼ cup (10 g) Thai basil leaves, cut into fine strips

1 Toss the cucumbers strips in with the salt and place in a colander to drain. Let it rest for 30 minutes (don't rinse). Squeeze out any excess moisture by squeezing the cucumbers with a towel.
2 While massaging gently, rinse the shallots under cool running water for 15 seconds—this will reduce the raw flavor, set aside.
3 Meanwhile, whisk together the vinegar, sugar, and fish sauce in a medium bowl. Fold in the salted cucumbers, shallots, ginger, chili, and basil. Taste and adjust seasoning with salt and/or sugar.

1 Cut the cucumbers lengthwise, creating sticks with angular ends.

2 Fold in the cucumbers, shallots, ginger, chili and basil.

Sriracha Chicken Salad

Before chilies, peppercorns were used to make Thai food spicy. Then in the 15ᵗʰ century the Portuguese brought chilies with them from the new world. If you can take the time to toast some peppercorns in a skillet until they begin to smoke, let them cool, then grind them fresh for this dish. Cooking your own chicken is another choice you can make; so many stores have roasted chicken ready it's hard to resist, especially on those days when you have no time—just keep in mind pre-roasted birds are seasoned and that will alter the final taste—reduce or omit the salt in the dressing to compensate. If pomelos are in season, add 1 cup (175 g) of segments to this salad. Using roasted rice powder to bind excess liquid and add a depth of flavor is a Thai technique I have become enamored with. Simply roast raw sticky rice (jasmine can work) slowly in dry skillet or wok until golden brown cool then grind fine

Serves 4–6
Preparation time: 15 mins + resting time
Cooking time: 25 mins

1 whole chicken (about 3–4 lb/1.25–1.5 kg)
½ cup (60 g) thinly sliced red onions, soaked in ice water for 15 minutes, drained well
½ cup (15 g) roughly chopped coriander leaves (cilantro)
¼ head green cabbage, cut into 2–4 wedges

CHILI-LIME DRESSING
2 teaspoons finely grated lime zest
6 tablespoons fresh lime juice
2 teaspoons coarsely ground black peppercorns
1 tablespoon Thai palm sugar or light brown sugar
2 tablespoons fish sauce
1–2 tablespoons Sriracha Chili Sauce (page 35)
2 tablespoons oil
1 tablespoon roasted rice powder (optional)

1 Buy a pre-roasted chicken and pull off the meat into bite-sized strip or poach a chicken in a 2-gallon (8-liter) pot, add enough water to cover the chicken. Bring to a vigorous boil; then lower the heat to simmer. Skim off any impurities that rise to the surface; simmer 15 minutes. Remove the pot from the heat; cover it. Allow it to rest at room temperature for 45 minutes, until the chicken reaches an internal temperature of 165°F (75°C).
2 Carefully lift the chicken from the poaching liquid and plunge it into ice water. Leave in the water for 10 minutes (this stops the cooking and firms up the meat). Pull off the skin and discard. Pull the meat from the breast, thighs, and legs, tearing it into bite-sized strips; set aside 1 lb (500 g) for the salad, save the remaining meat for another use. Transfer to a covered container and reserve in the refrigerator. (Save the poaching liquid (broth) for Thai curries or other recipes!)
3 Prepare the Chili-Lime Dressing by whisking all the ingredients in a large bowl.
4 Toss the onions, chicken, and coriander leaves into the dressing and mix it well. Taste and adjust seasoning with salt, pepper, sugar, and fresh lime juice.
5 Serve the salad in a large bowl or on a plate surrounded with the cabbage wedges, the wedges are meant for snacking on with the salad, adding a refreshing crunchy texture and slightly sweet taste.

Chapter Three
Meat and Poultry

I admit it, I don't think I'll ever become a vegetarian. I love nibbling on crispy tidbits of pork and even yanking the bubbling brown skin off freshly grilled chicken and devouring it while no one is looking. I respect folks that have chosen the path of being a vegetarian, whether it's for ethical, religious, or health reasons—I just can't do it myself. This chapter is dedicated to chicken, duck, pork, and beef and those recipes that feature these meats in all their delicious glory.

Thais have figured out how to create a balanced diet. One part of this equation is creating intensely flavorful meat and poultry dishes so that they can eat smaller amounts of meat while still enjoying the maximum amount of meaty flavor. Aromatic herb pastes flavor meats before they are slow roasted over a smoky charcoal fire. Coconut-spice paste enriched curries, and slowly simmered cauldrons of meat, spiked with soy and fish sauce will yield deeply satisfying flavors.

Proper cooking technique is as important as the quality of raw ingredients that you buy, so make sure to take a look at the Thai Cooking Tips chapter (page 22). Traveling in Thailand for the past twenty years has taught me so much. One of those major lessons is that Thais have their own unique way of cooking. Each country adapts their techniques to fit their culture, climate, and traditions. Here, I have shortened some of the traditional cooking times to avoid over cooking, cooking times are a bit different if you are making curries to sit in the tropical heat for hours. If you have years of cooking experience then use your instinct, but if you're unsure of what to do, just follow the recipes…they work.

Probably one of the best recipes to start with is the Red Curry Chicken (page 65), it's such a simple recipe and you will impress yourself with how well it comes out, even on your first try. I'll bet you like it more than what you find at the local Thai restaurant. Although most people think of stir-frying as a Chinese cooking technique, and there is some historical validity to this, the Thai's are very adept with a wok. Check out the Tamarind Soy Chicken with Cashews stir-fry (page 63), one of my favorite recipes in this chapter, the tamarind's uniquely sweet and tart flavor, aromatic basil leaves perfume the sauce and roasted cashews add a delightful crunch and rich flavor. When you are in the mood for your home to be filled with the sweet aroma of a simmering stew, then turn to Five Spice Slow-cooked Pork (page 66), the five spice mixture, garlic, and ginger aromas will fill the air, igniting the senses, inciting the appetite, and comforting the soul.

Stir-fried Pork with Basil and Chilies

This could be THE classic example of Thai street food—inexpensive to make, quick to prepare, and simply delicious. This version of *moo pad ka phrao* is usually made with ground pork, but you can use ground poultry or beef. If you can find them, use holy basil leaves for a truly authentic flavor. I just love when it's served with a fried egg on top, they cook it at a high-temperature and the result is a slightly crispy fried egg. Serve this with a mound of steamed rice and you have the makings of the perfect Thai meal.

Serves 4–6   Preparation time: 5 mins   Cooking time: 7 mins

2 tablespoons oil
3–6 Thai chilies, minced
2 tablespoons minced garlic
1½ lb (750 g) coarsely ground pork
4 teaspoons fish sauce
1 tablespoon oyster sauce
2 teaspoons dark soy sauce
1 teaspoon sugar
1 cup (30 g) Thai basil leaves

1 Heat a large skillet or wok over high heat. Swirl the oil in the skillet to coat the entire surface, and keep heating the skillet until it gets very hot and the oil begins to smoke.
2 Stir-fry the chilies and garlic until the garlic begins to brown, about 5–10 seconds. Stir in the ground pork and continue stir-frying, breaking up the pork as you cook it. Continue to cook until the pork is 75% cooked.
3 Stir-in the fish sauce, oyster sauce, soy sauce, and sugar and mix well to coat the meat with the sauces. Continue to cook until the sauce glazes the pork, about 30 seconds.
4 Toss in the basil until it wilts. Spoon into serving bowl or plate. If desired top with a fried egg and serve with steamed rice.

Tamarind Soy Chicken with Cashews

Tamarind Soy Chicken with Cashews

Richly flavored and aromatic from the Thai basil, this salty-sweet stir-fry will become one of your favorites. The sweet-n-sour tamarind pod hangs from large trees in Thailand, each fruit is filled with the gooey pulp that's mixed with water and strained creating the pulp that entices cultures around the world. You can decide how spicy you like it. Since each chili's heat varies I always nibble on the bit of the seed filled end to check the chili's spice before I decide on how many will fit my mood.

Serves 4
Preparation time: 10 mins + marinating time
Cooking time: 5 mins

2 boneless chicken breasts or 4 deboned thighs (about 12 oz/350 g) cut into bite-sized strips
1 tablespoon oyster sauce
1 tablespoon Thai palm sugar or light brown sugar
1 tablespoon minced garlic
1 tablespoon minced ginger
2–6 Thai chilies, minced
2 tablespoons oil (divided use)
2 cups (160 g) Chinese broccoli, cut into bite-sized pieces
1 cup (120 g) sliced red onions
1 tablespoon Tamarind Pulp or concentrate (page 25)
1 tablespoon sweet soy sauce
1 cup (30 g) Thai basil leaves
½ cup (75 g) roasted or fried cashews

1 Toss the chicken with the oyster sauce, sugar, garlic, ginger, chilies, and 1 tablespoon of the oil, then marinate for a minimum of 30 minutes at room temperature, or refrigerate for longer. Marinating overnight tenderizes the chicken.
2 Get organized to stir-fry by bringing the chicken to room temperature and organizing all the items in the order that they will go in the pan, this allows you to add things quickly! (See Stir-frying 101 on page 30.)
3 Heat a large skillet or wok over high heat. Swirl the remaining tablespoon of oil in the skillet to coat the entire surface, and keep heating the skillet until it is very hot and the oil begins to smoke.
4 Stir-fry the marinated chicken until 50% cooked, about 2-3 minutes. Add the broccoli and onions and stir-fry for 1 minute, then add the tamarind and soy sauce. Cook until the chicken and vegetables are coated and cooked through. Stir in the basil leaves and remove from the heat.
5 Taste and adjust the seasoning with tamarind, sweet soy, or oyster sauce as desired.
6 Spoon onto a serving platter and garnish with the cashews.

Grilled Lemongrass Chicken

The rural roads of the northeast Issan region of Thailand are filled with smoky grills packed with Grilled Lemongrass Chicken. This recipe will let you recreate this traditional dish on your grill at home. Always served with Thai Sweet Chili Sauce (Nahm Jim Gai) (page 35) for dipping, it's no wonder Thais love to feast on this street food.

Serves 4–6
Preparation time: 10 mins + marinating time
Cooking time: 20 mins

2 stalks lemongrass, tender inner part of bottom third only, very thinly sliced

2 teaspoons minced coriander stems (cilantro stems)

2–4 Thai chilies

1 teaspoon coarsely ground white peppercorns

3 tablespoons fish sauce

2 tablespoons Thai palm sugar or light brown sugar

6–8 chicken thighs or 3-4 legs, (bone-in) scored lightly with a knife to allow the marinade in

2 small cucumbers, cut into wedges

½ cup (125 ml) Thai Sweet Chili Sauce (page 35)

1 Make a coarse paste with the lemongrass, coriander stems, chilies, and peppercorns using a mortar and pestle or a mini-food processor.

2 Mix in the fish sauce and palm sugar until the sugar dissolves.

3 Coat the chicken with this spice paste and then marinate, refrigerate for at least one hour. Marinating chicken overnight always improves the flavor and tenderization.

4 Preheat the grill to medium-low heat. Slowly grill the chicken, turning often until cooked through and golden brown all over. Alternatively you can rotisserie, bake, or broil this chicken until cooked through to an internal temperature of 165°F (75°C).

5 Serve with wedges of cucumber to snack on and a bowl of Thai Sweet Chili Sauce for dipping.

1 Slice the lemongrass thinly.

2 Make a coarse paste with the lemongrass, coriander stems, chilies and peppercorns.

3 Score the chicken pieces, at the thickest part, lightly with a knife.

Red Curry Chicken

The sultry coconut curries of Thailand are addictive, once you try one, you will want to explore the rainbow of colors and flavors. Feel free to replace the red curry paste with other curry pastes such as yellow or Penang. You can also turn this into a full meal by adding pepper strips, bite-sized green or long beans and other vegetables to the sauce—just add some steamed rice and you are all set for a feast. Each brand of curry paste has varying levels of salt, so taste the curry after it's made and, if necessary, add some salt and/or sugar to taste. Thais often garnish red curries with a drizzle of coconut milk.

Serves 4–6
Preparation time: 5 mins
Cooking time: 10 mins

1²/₃ cups (400 ml) coconut milk (divided use)
¼ cup (65 ml) red curry paste
1 cup (250 ml) chicken or vegetable stock/broth
2 tablespoons Thai palm sugar or light brown sugar
1 teaspoon fish sauce
1 lb (500 g) boneless, skinless chicken thighs, cut into bite-sized strips
2 stalks lemongrass, tender inner part of bottom third only, bruised
6 kaffir lime leaves (substitute 1 teaspoon finely grated lime zest)
½ cup (15 g) Thai basil leaves

1 Heat ½ cup (125 ml) of the coconut milk in a small saucepan over medium-high heat. Cook, stirring constantly, until it reduces by about half and thickens considerably and begins to separate (about 5 minutes). Mix in the curry paste and cook for an additional minute.
2 Pour in the remaining coconut milk, stock, sugar, fish sauce, chicken, lemongrass, and kaffir lime leaves. Bring to a boil. Lower the heat to simmer for 3–5 minutes, until the chicken is cooked. Taste the sauce and adjust seasoning with fish sauce, salt, and/or sugar.
3 Stir in the basil leaves, remove from the heat and serve.

4 Grill the chicken until golden brown.

Serves 4–6
Preparation time: 10 mins
Cooking time: 3–4 hours

3 lb (1.25 kg) pork hocks, leg or
  shoulder, cut into 3 or 4 large
  pieces
6 cups (1.5 liter) pork, chicken, or
  vegetable stock
6 tablespoons sweet soy sauce
¼ cup (65 ml) oyster sauce
3 tablespoons fish sauce
¼ cup (10 g) chopped coriander
  stems (cilantro stems)
6 cloves garlic, smashed
1 teaspoon five spice powder
3-inch (7.5 cm) piece ginger,
  smashed
¼ teaspoon ground white pepper

1 Cover the pork with the stock, soy
sauce, oyster sauce, fish sauce, and
if necessary, add enough water to
cover the pork. Stir in the coriander
stems, garlic, five spice powder,
ginger, and white pepper.
2 Bring to a boil then lower the heat
to simmer and skim any scum that
rises to the surface. Cover and cook
on a very low heat (barely a simmer)
for 3–4 hours or until pork is very
tender. If using a pressure cooker
bring up to pressure and cook for 15
minutes
3 Taste the broth and adjust seasoning with soy sauce and sugar. Serve
with bowls of jasmine rice and some
vegetables for a complete meal.

Five Spice Slow-cooked Pork

This is one of the first things I eat when I go to Thailand where large cauldrons of
luscious sweet tender pork legs bathing in the star anise spiked broth are found in
local markets and food courts. The hocks (the bottom portion of the leg) and the
upper leg are often used with the fatty skin on. The skin is actually the most coveted
part of it since after simmer it becomes so soft and succulent. You may opt to use the
readily available pork shoulder, also called butt with its marbled meat. To save time,
I use a pressure cooker, if I am in no rush I sometimes use a slow cooker. So rich and
savory, I like to serve this with the Crunchy Sweet Papaya Pickles (page 42) or buy
some ready-made pickled mustard greens.

Serves 4–6
Preparation time: 10 mins
Cooking time: 10 mins

1²/₃ cups (400 ml) coconut milk (divided
  use)
¼ cup (65 ml) green curry paste
1 cup (250 ml) chicken, pork or vegetable
  stock/broth
2 tablespoons Thai palm sugar or light
  brown sugar
1 teaspoon fish sauce
1 lb (500 g) pork, (shoulder, leg, or other
  cut), sliced into thin bite-sized pieces
2 stalks lemongrass, tender inner part of
  bottom third only, bruised
6 kaffir lime leaves (substitute 1 teaspoon
  finely grated lime zest)
2 cups (100 g) sliced eggplant (Japanese,
  Chinese or Thai)
¼ cup (10 g) coarsely chopped coriander
  leaves (cilantro)

1 Heat ½ cup of the coconut milk in a small
saucepan over medium-high heat. Cook,
stirring constantly, until it reduces by about
half and thickens considerably (about 5
minutes). Mix in the curry paste and cook
for an additional minute.
2 Pour in the remaining coconut milk, stock,
sugar, fish sauce, pork, lemongrass, and
kaffir lime leaves, then stir in the eggplant
and bring to a boil. Lower the heat to
simmer for 3–5 minutes until the pork and
eggplant is cooked. Taste the sauce and
adjust seasoning with fish sauce, salt and/
or sugar.
3 Remove from the heat, transfer to a serving bowl and garnish with the coriander
leaves.

Green Curry Pork with Eggplant

This is one of the spicier curry pastes you'll find, so get ready for the sweet heat
of Thai flavors! Silky eggplant pieces and slivers of tender pork are traditional
partners in the Thai kitchen. As with all of the coconut curries in this book, I
like to add the whole kaffir lime leaves (or zest) and lemongrass to fortify the
pre-made curry paste; if you don't have them go ahead and make the curry and
you'll still end up with delicious results.

Chapter Four
Seafood

Sterling fresh seafood is a hallmark of Thai cooking, and these recipes celebrate the natural sweet flavors of these aquatic creatures. You can choose to fire up a stir-fry, simmer a curry, toss a fresh salad, or light up the grill. With seafood, the quality of your raw ingredients is essential. There's a strategy I learned while shopping in the markets of Southeast Asia: always buy your seafood first. It may seem counterintuitive to buy your seafood first because you don't want to carry it around, and I don't. So this is what I do: I head to the seafood department first and pick out my selection. Finding the choicest cuts, the sweetest shrimp, the most tender squid, brightest red gills on fish, then I pay for it, have it packed up, and, very importantly, have them keep it on, in, or under ice for me while I continue to shop. Then I come back when I'm done shopping for all my other items. Doing it this way helps me decide what I'm going to cook. Don't forget to ask for a bag of ice to pack with your fish for your ride home (yes, you can even do this at supermarkets), even a few degrees difference will transform brilliantly fresh seafood into a poor quality seafood—KEEP IT COLD!

Can frozen seafood be fresher that fresh? Yes. Candidly some frozen seafood is "fresher" than fresh, "huh" you may say. This is the deal. Frozen seafood is often frozen right after catching it, and, if done with proper techniques, the quality can be very high. "Fresh" seafood could have been caught, packed, shipped, warehoused, shipped to the market…you get the idea, it could be a week from the time it leaves the water until it arrives on your plate, and often I would prefer high quality frozen seafood that's defrosted and eaten right away. Probably 95% of the shrimp you've ever eaten was previously frozen. It is important to defrost it slowly (overnight) in the refrigerator. Try to plan ahead, avoid submerging the exposed seafood in water, the direct contact washes out much of its flavor and ruins its texture. If you are in a rush put it in a sealed bag and let the slow cool running water pour over it to speed up the defrosting process.

Some of my favorites in this chapter include the Garlic Crab with Green Beans (page 76) its simplicity is only surpassed by its yum factor. BBQ Fish in Red Curry Spices (page 78) recipe will show you how easy it is to use these natural leaves, once you try this you will see how easy it would be to make endless variations. It can be as simple as using different colored curry paste or even making up your own spice marinade based on what you have around. Fire-roasted Shrimp (page 74) are great when you want to get things ready ahead of time, just pop them in the broiler for a few minutes and you're ready to eat.

Grilled Catfish with a Tangy Glaze

The first time I tasted a tamarind glazed deep-fried whole fish I was hooked! It is rare though for most of us to deep-fry an entire fish at home and grilled fish redolent of smoky coals is also amazing. …don't forget though that most large Asian markets will clean and fry a fish for you…for free. Make this sweet and sour topping before you go shopping, then bring that crispy fish home, drench it in this glaze, garnish, and you'll have an impressive feast.

Serves 4–6
Preparation time: 10 mins
Cooking time: 15 mins

¼ cup (75 g) Thai palm sugar or light
    brown sugar
1 tablespoon fish sauce
2 tablespoons Tamarind Pulp or
    concentrate (page 25)
2 shallots, thinly sliced
1–2 Thai chilies, minced
1 teaspoon minced ginger
1 teaspoon fresh lime juice
1 tablespoon chopped coriander
    leaves (cilantro)
4–6 catfish fillets (about 1 lb/500 g)
    or one whole catfish (about
    2–3 lb/1–1.25 kg), cleaned and
    gutted
1 tablespoon oil
¼ cup (5 g) mint leaves
1 tablespoon Fried Garlic (page 37)

1 Stir together the palm sugar, fish sauce and tamarind in a small saucepan and bring to a boil over medium heat for 1 minute until it is a smooth syrup. Stir in the shallots and remove from the heat. Allow to cool to room temperature, then mix in the chilies, ginger, lime juice, and coriander leaves. Set aside at room temperature or store in refrigerator for later while you prepare the fish.

2 Preheat the grill or oven broiler until very hot. Make sure to clean the grill well, then wipe the grill grates lightly with oil. Grill the fish until cooked through, if using a whole fish, grill over medium-low heat until cooked through (sometimes I like to wrap the fish in a banana leaf before grilling to infuse its illusive aroma). Alternately you can pan-fry or sauté the fish in a skillet or wok.

3 Arrange the fish on a plate or platter, spoon the sauce over the fish (serve the extra sauce on the side in a small bowl). Sprinkle the fish with the mint leaves and Fried Garlic.

Yellow Curry Shrimp

Yellow Curry Shrimp

Brilliant yellows, bright flavors, and tender shrimp come together in this harmonious Thai curry, and to think that you could have this on the table in 30 minutes any day of the week! Once you buy the curry paste it's a snap to whip up curries on a moment's notice, and don't be shy about experimenting with different vegetables and seafood—chicken would also have a home here. Take the 5 minutes to create the toasty coconut oil before roasting the curry paste to its full potential.

Serves 4–6
Preparation time: 5 mins
Cooking time: 15 mins

1²/₃ cups (400 ml) coconut milk (divided use)
¼ cup (65 ml) yellow or sour curry paste
1 cup (250 ml) chicken, seafood or vegetable stock/broth
2 tablespoons Thai palm sugar or light brown sugar
1 teaspoon fish sauce
2 stalks lemongrass, tender inner part of bottom third only, bruised
6 kaffir lime leaves (substitute 1 teaspoon finely grated lime zest)
1 lb (500 g) peeled and deveined raw shrimp
1 cup (130 g) unripe papaya (substitute chayote) peeled and sliced into bite-sized pieces
¼ cup (10 g) roughly chopped coriander leaves (cilantro)
2 red finger-length chilies, cut into small strips or thin rings

1 Heat ½ cup (125 ml) of the coconut milk in a small saucepan over medium-high heat. Cook, stirring constantly, until it reduces by about half and thickens considerably (about 5 minutes). Mix in the curry paste and cook for an additional minute.
2 Pour in the remaining coconut milk, stock, sugar, fish sauce, lemongrass, and kaffir lime leaves, and bring to a boil. Lower the heat to simmer for 3 minutes to infuse the sauce with the aromatics. Add the shrimp and papaya and continue to simmer for 2–5 minutes until cooked through. Taste the sauce and adjust seasoning with fish sauce, salt and/or sugar.
3 Remove from the heat, stir in the coriander leaves and transfer into serving bowls and garnish with the chilies.

Fire-roasted Shrimp

Jumbo shrimp, split open and slathered with a chili enriched savory glaze, crusts these shrimp as they broil to perfection in just a few minutes. I really prefer the texture of hand minced ingredients in the topping, but if you don't have or are simply not in the mood, you can use a mini-food processor to chop the ingredients into a coarse paste. They are added in different stages so chop the garlic and bean paste together in one batch, then a separate batch of lemongrass, chilies, and ginger. If you can't find the yellow bean paste you could substitute with brown bean paste or light brown Japanese miso paste. In Thailand these are best when served with the heads still on, split down the middle so you can pick out all the tasty bits.

Serves 4–6
Preparation time: 20 mins
Cooking time: 12 mins

¼ cup (65 ml) oil
2 tablespoons yellow bean paste (if beans are large, chop or mash them well)
3 tablespoons minced garlic
¼ cup (25 g) finely minced lemongrass, tender inner part of bottom third only
¼ cup (25 g) minced red finger-length chilies
2 tablespoons minced ginger
1 tablespoon Thai palm sugar or light brown sugar
¼ cup (60 g) minced green onions (scallions)
2 tablespoons oyster sauce
1 teaspoon ground black pepper
12–18 large shrimp with shells intact, about 2 lbs (1 kg)
6–8 coriander (cilantro) sprigs
2 limes, cut into wedges

1 Stir the oil, bean paste and garlic together in a small saucepan over medium heat, cook until the garlic is cooked and loses its sharp flavor, about 3 minutes.
2 Mix in the lemongrass, chilies, and ginger, and cook for an additional 2 minutes. Then add the sugar, green onions, oyster sauce, and black pepper. Remove from the heat. Continue to stir until the palm sugar is dissolved. Transfer to a bowl and taste, adjust seasoning with chilies, sugar, and oyster sauce.
3 Preheat the broiler to high, place one oven/broiler rack as close as possible to the burners.
4 Split the shrimp along the top of the shell to butterfly them. Arrange on a baking sheet and divide the lemongrass mixture among all the shrimp, spread on the shrimp to coat somewhat evenly. Broil on high heat until the mixture begins to brown and the shrimp are cooked through, about 3–5 minutes. I tend to rotate them half way through so they will cook evenly.
5 Arrange the shrimp on a platter, garnish with the coriander sprigs and serve with wedges of lime.

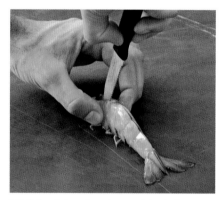

1 Split the shrimp along the top of the shell to butterfly it.

2 Divide the lemongrass mixture among the shrimp.

Garlic Crab with Green Beans

This flavorful dish comes together in minutes with remarkable results. My Thai cuisine mentors, Khun Ning and Kobkeaw Nijpinij of Khao Cooking School, showed me this recipe at a restaurant in Bangkok. Although freshly simmered and plucked crab is wonderful, it's time consuming to make, so I usually splurge on premium refrigerated cooked crabmeat. They use spicy orange chilies, but they can be difficult to find so I tend to use finger-length red chilies or red Fresno chilies—and after chopping them I like to pound them slightly in a mortar so they release more of their flavor into the oil, if you don't have a mortar simply smash them slightly with the side of a knife.

Serves 4–6
Preparation time: 5 mins
Cooking time: 7 mins

¼ cup (65 ml) oil
2 cloves garlic, finely minced
1 cup (100 g) long beans or green beans, ends trimmed, sliced into pieces
½ cup (50 g) roughly chopped red finger-length chilies, smashed lightly
1 teaspoon fish sauce
½ teaspoon sugar
1 lb (500 g) lump crabmeat, picked through for shells

1 Combine the oil, garlic, green beans, and chilies in a medium skillet or wok and heat over medium-low heat while stirring and cook for about 1 minute or until the beans are just cooked through (do not brown the garlic).
2 Mix in the fish sauce and the sugar until dissolved.
3 Gently toss in the crabmeat and heat until just warmed through.
4 Transfer to a plate and serve with steamed rice.

Sweet-and-Sour Shrimp

This is not your typical cloying sweet-n-sour dish, these black pepper marinated shrimp are enrobed by tamarind-lime glaze. Green beans, bell peppers, broccoli, hearty Asian greens, or other favorites can be used instead of the seasonal asparagus. When I make this for dinner I add a few minced Thai chilies for some heat, steam a pot of Jasmine Rice (page 102) and I am set for a quick meal.

**Serves 4–6   Preparation time: 10 mins + marinating time
Cooking time: 12 mins**

12 oz (350 g) medium shrimp, peeled and deveined
2 teaspoons fish sauce
1 teaspoon sugar
½ teaspoon ground black pepper
2 tablespoons oil (divided use)
½ cup (65 g) thickly sliced shallots
1 tablespoon minced ginger
1 cup (120 g) asparagus, large bite-sized pieces
3 tablespoons Thai sweet chili sauce
2 tablespoons Tamarind Pulp or concentrate (page 25)
2 tablespoons fresh lime juice
½ cup (40 g) green onions (scallions), large bite-sized pieces
½ cup (75 g) cherry or grape tomatoes, cut in halves
¼ cup (10 g) chopped coriander leaves (cilantro)

1 Toss the shrimp with the fish sauce, sugar, pepper, and 1 tablespoon of the oil, then marinate for a minimum of 30 minutes at room temperature, or refrigerate for longer. Marinating shrimp overnight tenderizes the shrimp.
2 Get organized to stir-fry by bringing the shrimp to room temperature and organizing all the items in the order that they will go in the skillet, this allows you to add things quickly!
3 Heat a large skillet or wok over high heat. Swirl the remaining tablespoon of oil in the skillet to coat the entire surface, and heat the skillet until the oil begins to smoke.
4 Stir in the shrimp, shallots, ginger, and stir-fry until the shrimp are 50% cooked, about 2 minutes. Add the asparagus and stir-fry for 1 minute. Cook until the shrimp and asparagus are almost cooked through.
5 Mix in the sweet chili sauce, tamarind, lime juice, and green onions, and stir until coated. Stir in the tomatoes and coriander leaves, and remove from the heat.
6 Taste and adjust seasoning with tamarind, lime juice, sugar, fish sauce, or salt.
7 Spoon onto a serving platter and serve with bowls of steamed Jasmine Rice.

BBQ Fish in Red Curry Spices

Unwrapping a steaming piece of just-grilled fish is like opening a gift. I created this dish for a Fourth of July gathering. Fortunately, it's so easy to make the packets ahead of time! When it was time to eat, I quickly grilled the aromatic red curry fish wrapped with smoky banana leaves packets then they could add the final touches by drizzling the coconut milk, coriander leaves (cilantro), and chili slices over the fish to their liking.

Serves 4–6
Preparation time: 15 mins + marinating time
Cooking time: 10 mins

2 tablespoons red curry paste
¾ cup (180 ml) coconut milk (divided use)
1 teaspoon fish sauce
1 tablespoon rice flour (substitute with cornstarch)
1 tablespoon Thai palm sugar or light brown sugar
¼ teaspoon sea salt or kosher salt
4 kaffir lime leaves
1½ lb (750 g) fish fillets—cod, snapper, catfish—sliced into strips about ½-inch (1.25 cm) thick
4–6 pieces banana leaves, cut into about 16-inch (40 cm) square pieces
½ cup (15 g) Thai basil leaves
¼ cup (10 g) coriander leaves (cilantro)
1 red finger-length chili, thinly sliced
2 limes, cut into wedges

1 To marinate the fish, whisk the curry paste, ½ cup (125 ml) of the coconut milk, fish sauce, rice flour, palm sugar, and salt together in a large bowl until smooth. Stir in the kaffir lime leaves. Toss the fish in this mixture until coated well to ensure even seasoning.

2 To assemble the packets: On a clean work-surface, arrange a banana leaf (shiny side down) with the natural line patterns running from left to right (horizontally). Place about four Thai basil leaves in the center of the bottom ¼ of the leaf. Top the basil with 4–6 slices of fish per package, shingling them tightly. Gently, yet tightly, roll the fish in the banana leaf, creating several layers around fish. There should be about 3 inches (7.5 cm) of banana leaf extended past the fish, which you will fold over the top and towards the center, securing it with toothpicks or skewers.

3 Cook the fish on a preheated grill, griddle, or skillet over medium heat, grill the packets for 3–5 minutes on each side, until the leaf is lightly-charred and fish is cooked through. If in doubt about doneness you can use an instant read thermometer and look for 135°F/57°C reading.

4 To serve, carefully open the packets, drizzle with the remaining coconut milk and sprinkle with coriander leaves and chilies. Serve with lime wedges.

1 Fold over the top and towards the center.

Squid with Cilantro and Mint

This dish is so simple it is best served as part of a larger meal instead of the central dish. Although cuttlefish and squid (often called calamari) are technically different cephalopods, either one can work in this recipe, here I use the more commonly found small tender squid and they cook in seconds. Using cuttlefish may require you to cut them into small slivers and then also cook them briefly so they do not get too tough.

Serves 4–6
Preparation time: 10 mins
Cooking time: 5 mins

12 oz (350 g) cleaned squid, bodies
    cut into ½-inch (1.25 cm) rings and
    tentacles into bite-sized pieces
1 tablespoon oil
2 tablespoons minced coriander stems
    (cilantro stems)
2–4 Thai chilies, minced
3 cloves garlic, minced
1 teaspoon coarsely ground black
    peppercorns
1 tablespoon fish sauce
1 teaspoon sugar
¼ cup (10 g) chopped coriander leaves
    (cilantro)
½ cup (10 g) mint leaves

1 Get organized to stir-fry by bringing the squid to room temperature and organizing all the items in the order that they go in the skillet, this allows you to add things quickly! Make sure to dry the squid well so the sauce stays concentrated.
2 Heat a large skillet or wok over high heat. Swirl the oil in the skillet to coat the entire surface, and keep heating the skillet until very hot and the oil begins to smoke.
3 Stir fry the coriander stems, chilies, garlic, and pepper until aromatic and the garlic is beginning to become a golden brown (not dark brown), about 15 seconds.
4 Add the squid, fish sauce, and sugar and stir-fry until the squid is cooked, this is very brief, about 10–15 seconds! 5 Remove from the heat, toss in the coriander leaves and mint leaves. Spoon into a bowl.

2 Secure the ends with toothpicks.

Serves 4
Preparation time: 15 mins
Cooking time: 10 mins

¼ cup (30 g) thinly sliced red onions, soaked in ice
    water for 15 minutes, drained well
½ cup (60 g) thinly sliced cucumber (seeds removed)
1 cup (150 g) halved cherry tomatoes
3 cups (750 ml) water
1 teaspoon sea salt or kosher salt
1 lb (500 g) cleaned squid, bodies cut into ¼-inch (6
    mm) rings and tentacles into bite-sized pieces
¼ cup (10 g) roughly chopped coriander leaves
    (cilantro)

CHILI-LIME DRESSING
4 kaffir lime leaves (substitute 1 teaspoons finely
grated lime zest)
3 tablespoons fresh lime juice
1 stalk lemongrass, tender inner part of bottom third
    only, minced
1 tablespoon chili paste in soya bean oil (*nahm prik
    pow*)
1 tablespoon Thai palm sugar or light brown sugar
1 tablespoon fish sauce
1 teaspoon distilled white vinegar
Pinch of sea salt or kosher salt

1 Prepare the Chili-Lime Dressing by whisking all the
ingredients together in a large bowl until the chili paste
is dissolved. Set aside.
2 Toss the onions, cucumber and the cherry tomatoes
with the dressing.
3 Bring the water with the salt to a boil in a large saucepan. Remove from the heat, add the squid and stir for 10
seconds then drain well in a colander and briefly rinse
with cool tap water. Use paper towels to dry thoroughly.
4 Stir the squid in with the marinated vegetables. Add
the coriander leaves and toss to combine. Serve immediately.

Lime Cilantro Squid

This recipe is a brilliant example of the vibrantly flavored seafood
dishes of Thailand where a light non-fat dressing accentuates the
delicate flavors of the squid. Use whatever seafood looks best at the
market that day and feel free to substitute the squid with other seafood favorites like shrimp, scallops, or even lobster. Soaking the onions
in ice water reduces the "bite" of the raw onions and also gives it an
extra crisp texture.

Steamed Clams with Chili and Basil

Serves 4–6
Preparation time: 5 mins
Cooking time: 5 mins

2-3 lb (1-1.25 kg) small clams, washed very well
¼ cup (65 g) chili paste in soya bean oil (*nahm prik pow*)
6 kaffir lime leaves (substitute 1 teaspoon finely grated lime zest)
2 stalks lemongrass, tender inner part of bottom third only, smashed
2 tablespoons fish sauce
½ cup (125 ml) young coconut juice or water
1 cup (30 g) Thai basil leaves

1 Stir the clams, chili paste, kaffir lime leaves, lemongrass, fish sauce and coconut water together in a large saucepan. Place over high heat, cover and cook for about 2 minutes until the clams begin to open, remove the cover and stir constantly until all of the clams open—discard those that do not open (they were already dead and may be filled with mud).
2 Once all the clams are open, stir in the basil leaves. Taste and adjust seasoning of broth with salt.
3 Pile the clams in a bowl with the broth and serve with spoons and rice to savor the flavorful broth.

This popular street food is one that you can recreate with ease! I have taken the liberty to add young coconut water as a variation since it rounds out the flavor and adds a slightly sweet taste that is usually achieved with sugar. A pile of steamed rice is usually with this flavorful broth, but a non-traditional loaf of bread also works to soak up every drop of aromatic goodness.

Chapter Five

Vegetables

Vegetables provide a rainbow of colors, textures, and tastes, creating the most diverse flavor library of any category of ingredients in the world. Deep green long beans, bright red chilies, seductively purple eggplant, and rich brown mushrooms are only the beginning. Try adding some bean curd "tofu," serve with some noodles or rice and you're all set. Keep in mind that these recipes can be adjusted to include meat or seafood, my recipes are only guidelines and I hope that they continue to evolve in your kitchen.

Who are vegetarians anyway? This term has become watered down, and so many others have been created to help people fit in to today's society—flexitarian (those that abstain from meat certain meals or days), pescatarian (one who only eat seafood in addition to vegetables and fruit)…and the list goes on!

To me, there are really only two types of vegetarians: Vegans, those that consume no animal products whatsoever, not even honey; then the more common lacto-ovo vegetarians who choose to eat eggs and dairy products, often due to the fact that these items do not involve harming the animal. Of course, each person adheres to the rules with different degrees of fervor. There is no reason that it has to be all or nothing. I actually abstain from meat, poultry, or seafood for some meals but this chapter is not about abstinence, its about inclusion!

I suggest you begin with the Fire-roasted Eggplant (page 84) its profound smoky flavor and endless possibilities of vegetables to dip in it makes it one of my favorites. The Aromatic Thai Omelet (page 89) is a dish that I eat late at night on the streets of Bangkok or in homes as a quick dish to round out a meal, when I'm in the U.S., I love this for breakfast, with some Sriracha Chili Sauce (page 35) it's a great, savory way to start the day. Want a straight forward side dish? The Garlic Soy Mushrooms (page 86) is one of my favorites.

Go now, shop for some fresh produce at your local farmers market, Asian specialty store, or mainstream supermarket and try some of these amazing produce based recipes.

Fire-roasted Eggplant

This hauntingly addictive smoky fire-roasted relish can be scooped up with nearly anything—fresh veggies as described below, or grab a bag of chips and start scooping. Thai relishes, *nahm prik*, play a supporting roll to the rest of the meal. I have used fish sauce instead of the pungent more often used shrimp paste, *gkapi*. For an in depth look at *nahm prik* variations look to David Thompson's essential book, *Thai Food*.

Serves 4–6
Preparation time: 7 mins
Cooking time: 15 mins

4 Chinese or Japanese long eggplants
   (about 1½ lb/750 g)
4 red finger-length chilies
4 shallots, not peeled
6 cloves garlic, not peeled
2 tablespoons fresh lime juice
2 tablespoons fish sauce or soy sauce
1 teaspoon sugar
2 tablespoons chopped coriander leaves
   (cilantro)

RAW VEGETABLES FOR DIPPING—choose
   a few of the following
Cucumber slices
Green cabbage wedges
Long beans or green beans
Thai small green eggplant wedges
Asparagus

1 Grill the eggplants, chilies, shallots and garlic until charred and cooked through or arrange all on a baking sheet, place under preheated broiler on the highest setting with rack as close as possible to burner.

Broil until everything is semi-charred and cooked through. Cool to room temperature. Peel off the skin and charred surface.

2 Transfer the chilies, shallots, and garlic to a mortar or food processor and processed to a semi-smooth paste.

3 Roughly chop the eggplants with a knife and combine in a bowl with the chili mixture. Season with the lime juice, fish sauce, sugar, and coriander leaves. Taste and adjust seasoning with fish sauce and lime juice—it should be salty-sour and spicy.

4 Serve in a bowl with the Raw Vegetables For Dipping, ornately arranged.

1 Arrange the eggplant, chilies, shallots, and garlic on a baking sheet and grilled until charred.

2 Process the chiles, shallots, and garlic to a semi-smooth paste.

Grilled Tofu Curry

Tofu, a canvas for other intense flavors, revels in a bath of deep red spicy co-conut curry. When walking through Bangkok's Chinatown, yellow stained tofu pouches are stamped with red Chinese characters highlighting the maker of the tofu, a quick brush of turmeric lends a vivid yellow color. Buy the firm or extra-firm tofu that is packed in water, you may want to slice them before grilling.

Serves 4–6
Preparation time: 10 mins
Cooking time: 20 mins

1 lb (500 g) firm tofu (about 4–6 pieces)—drained and dried well
½ teaspoon sea salt or kosher salt
2 tablespoons oil
¼ teaspoon turmeric powder
1 cup (250 ml) coconut milk (divided use)
2 tablespoons red curry paste
¼ cup (65 ml) vegetable stock/broth
1 tablespoon Thai palm sugar or light brown sugar
1 teaspoon fish sauce or soy sauce
1 cup (120 g) fresh peas (substitute sliced snow peas)
1 cup (100 g) red bell peppers, sliced into strips
1 tablespoon fresh lime juice
½ cup (15 g) Thai basil leaves
3 kaffir lime leaves, vein removed, cut into very thin slivers (substitute 1 teaspoon finely grated lime zest)
1 tablespoon minced coriander stems (cilantro stems)

1 Sprinkle the tofu evenly with the salt. Whisk the oil and turmeric together in a small bowl, then use this mixture to brush on all surfaces of the tofu. Set aside.

2 Heat ¼ cup (65 ml) of the coconut milk in a small saucepan or skillet over medium-high heat. Cook, stirring constantly, until it reduces by about half and thickens considerably and begins to separate (about 3 minutes). Mix in the curry paste and cook for an additional minute. Pour in the remaining coconut milk, the stock, sugar, and soy sauce, and bring to a boil. Lower the heat to simmer for 5 minutes. Taste the sauce and adjust seasoning with soy sauce, salt and/or sugar.

3 Preheat grill or oven broiler until very hot. Make sure to clean the grill well, then wipe the grill grates lightly with oil. Grill the tofu, creating deep grill marks on both sides, you could also simply sauté the tofu until golden brown. Arrange in a wide bowl, or on a plate with steep sides, to hold the sauce.

4 Stir the peas and bell peppers into the curry. Simmer for 30 seconds, add the lime juice and stir in the basil leaves until wilted. Spoon the curry over and around the grilled tofu. Garnish with kaffir lime leaf slivers and coriander stems.

3 Combine the chili mixture with the chopped eggplant.

Garlic Soy Mushrooms

I discovered this simple stir-fry at David Thompson's Michelin Star rated London restaurant, Nahm, the most sophisticated Thai restaurant kitchen I have ever visited. There they use the large king oyster mushrooms, also found in the USA by the names of eryngii or king trumpet mushrooms. Another key ingredient to this dish is the yellow bean paste and if you haven't used this yet, you'll be surprised by the great taste. The readily available Chinese brown bean sauce or Japanese brown miso can be used as a substitute. Originally coriander (cilantro) root, ginger, and garlic were pounded into a rough paste with a mortar and pestle, this is still the best way to bring out the internal essence of the ingredients but a food processor will also work or just mince with a knife.

Serves 4–6
Preparation time: 5 mins
Cooking time: 5 mins

½ lb (250 g) oyster mushrooms, (divided use)
2 tablespoons minced coriander stems (cilantro stems) (about ¼ bunch)
1 tablespoon minced ginger
4 cloves of garlic, peeled
2 tablespoons yellow bean paste (if beans are large, chop or mash them well)
4 tablespoons oil (divided use)
2-inch (5 cm) ginger, sliced into thin matchsticks
4 green onions (scallions), cut into lengths
2 tablespoons chicken stock or water
¼ teaspoon sugar
Pinch of ground white pepper
Pinch of sea salt or kosher salt

1 Cut off any hard stem ends. Pull apart or cut into bite-sized pieces.
2 Grind the coriander stems, ginger, garlic, and bean paste to a paste in a mortar and pestle or mini food processor.
3 Heat a large skillet or wok over high heat. Swirl 1 tablespoon of the oil in the skillet to coat the entire surface, and keep heating the skillet until very hot and the oil begins to smoke. Toss in half the mushrooms and stir-fry for about 10 seconds until they are semi-cooked and have brown edges. Transfer the mushrooms to a bowl and set aside. Wipe out the skillet with a paper towel and repeat the process using another tablespoon of oil and the remaining half of the mushrooms. Reserve with the other mushrooms. Clean out the skillet again.
4 Reheat the skillet over high heat. Coat the skillet with the remaining 2 tablespoons of oil, then stir in the ground garlic mixture and cook for 10 seconds, then stir in the sliced ginger and green onions, and cook until the onions brighten in color. Add the stock, sugar, and pepper, and bring to a boil, simmer until a thick sauce is created. Toss the mushrooms into the sauce and stir to coat the mushrooms with the sauce for about 30 seconds to reheat. Season to taste with the salt and pepper, and serve immediately.

1 Small mushrooms are left whole, larger ones are pulled into bite-sized pieces.

Asian Greens with Roasted Garlic

Deep roasted flavors of garlic mingle with fresh greens in this almost instant side dish. The technique of starting with a cool pan allows you to achieve a rich flavored browned garlic without the bitter edge you might get with high heat cooking. You can use vegetarian stir-fry sauce for a vegetarian version. Choose whatever Asian greens available, I like the tender leaves and stems of choy sum yet the hearty stems and thick leaves of Chinese broccoli or the soft white stems and verdant leaves of bok choy are also welcomed to this flavorful party!

Serves 4–6
Preparation time: 5 mins
Cooking time: 5 mins

4 teaspoons oil or rendered pork fat
2 tablespoons chopped garlic
1 lb (500 g) choy sum or bok choy, sliced into large bite-sized pieces
1 tablespoon oyster sauce or vegetarian stir-fry sauce
1/8 teaspoon ground white pepper

1 Combine the oil and garlic in a large skillet, saucepan or wok at room temperature. Heat over low-medium heat and stir constantly while cooking the garlic until it is a golden brown.
2 Add the greens, increase the heat to high and cook, stirring constantly until the greens are wilted and just cooked. Stir in the oyster sauce and pepper.
3 Arrange in a bowl and serve hot or at room temperature.

2 If the beans are large, chop or mash them well.

3 Grind the coriander stems, ginger, garlic, and bean paste to a paste.

Silky Steamed Tofu with Caramelized Garlic Sauce

Serves 4–6   Preparation time: 5 mins   Cooking time: 15 mins

A large silky cube of tofu is elevated to top culinary status with slivers of browned garlic and a kaffir lime leaf infused sauce. Steaming the tofu and greens is a simple way to reheat the tofu and cook the greens at the same time. Silken tofu usually comes in "aseptic packaging" that does not require refrigeration until opening, it is delicate so be cautious taking it out of the package. I suggest, trimming off one corner, then one narrow end—this releases the tofu and it can slide right out.

2 tablespoons oil (divided use)
1 cup (40 g) sliced fresh shiitake or oyster mushrooms, stems removed
About 1 lb (500 g) silken soft tofu (package size varies—use two if needed)
2 cups (100 g) spinach, watercress or other tender greens
2 tablespoons thinly sliced garlic
¼ cup (65 ml) vegetable or chicken stock
2 tablespoons soy sauce
1 teaspoon sugar
½ teaspoon dried red chili flakes or ground dried red finger-length chilies
½ cup (120 g) chopped green onions (scallions)
3 kaffir lime leaves or ½ teaspoon finely grated lime zest
¼ cup (20 g) Fried Shallots (page 37)

1 Heat a large skillet or wok over medium heat, add 1 tablespoon of the oil, stir-fry the mushrooms until wilted and beginning to brown on the edges. Remove and reserve.

2 Gently remove the tofu from the package. Make a bed of greens on a large plate with rimmed edges (so the delicious sauce is contained), then place the tofu on top of the greens in the center of the plate. Steam for 8–10 minutes or gently microwave about 4 minutes until the greens are wilted and tofu is warmed through.

3 Heat a large skillet or wok over medium heat, add the remaining oil, then stir in the garlic and fry over medium heat until the garlic is golden brown. Immediately add the stock to stop the cooking, stir in the mushrooms and soy sauce, sugar, chilies, green onions, and kaffir lime leaves. Bring to a boil, taste and adjust seasoning with soy sauce—sauce should be strong since tofu is not seasoned.

4 Re-warm then pour the sauce over the warmed tofu. Sprinkle with the Fried Shallots.

Aromatic Thai Omelet

Sometimes I just want to make something quick to eat, and, in Thailand, cooks rely on simple recipes like this Aromatic Thai Omelet to provide sustenance for only pennies a portion. I have devoured versions of Thai omelets on the streets of Bangkok, the homes of the central plains of Thailand and in my home kitchen. This is a very flexible recipe, so go ahead and add ingredients you enjoy, such as strips of mushrooms, chopped carrots, Asian greens, or other tidbits you have in the refrigerator. Here is an opportunity to celebrate the season and incorporate what screams freshness at the market.

Serves 4–6
Preparation time: 6 mins
Cooking time: 5 mins

4 large eggs
1 tablespoon fish sauce
1 stalk lemongrass, tender inner part of bottom third only, minced
1 clove garlic, minced
¼ cup (25 g) chopped long beans or green beans
1 red finger-length chili, minced
1 green onion (scallion), chopped
1 tablespoon chopped coriander leaves (cilantro)
Pinch of sea salt or kosher salt
2 tablespoons oil

1 Whisk all ingredients (except the oil) together until smooth.
2 Heat a small non-stick skillet or wok over high heat, add the oil and heat until just smoking, about 30 seconds.
3 Pour the egg mixture into the skillet, the edges will bubble up but that's okay! Stir constantly until some of the egg is cooked but there is still some of the liquid from the eggs left (10 seconds). Stop stirring and cook for 2 minutes until the bottom is light brown and it's cooked enough to flip.
4 Flip the omelet using a spatula to aid you if you need to, then cook it on the second side until it's light brown and cooked through.
5 Slide out onto a plate and garnish with coriander leaves, if desired. Serve with your favorite chili sauce.

Mussaman Potato Curry

Serves 4–6
Preparation time: 10 mins
Cooking time: 20 mins

Sweet spices perfume this creamy Southern Style curry with roasted peanuts simmered in the coconut-laden sauce. The use of cinnamon, cloves, cardamom, and nutmeg in the curry paste showcases the influence that Indian and Malay food have on the flavors of Southern Thailand. Although this recipe doesn't have any meat, it is originally made with beef, it's best to simmer the beef with some coconut milk and stock ahead of time, then fold it in with the potatoes and adjust the seasoning as needed.

1²/₃ cups (400 ml) coconut milk (divided use)
¼ cup (70 g) Mussaman curry paste
1 cup (250 ml) vegetable or chicken stock/broth
1 stick cinnamon, about 3 inch (7.5 cm) long
1 teaspoons grated ginger
2 tablespoons Thai palm sugar or light brown sugar
2 teaspoons fish sauce or soy sauce
1 tablespoon Tamarind Pulp or concentrate (page 25)
1 cup (120 g) onions, bite-sized pieces
5-6 medium "waxy" potatoes like Yukon gold, red bliss or white rose, cut into large bite-sized pieces
¾ cup (100 g) roasted or deep-fried peanuts
1 cup (50 g) oyster mushrooms, larger ones are pulled into bite-sized pieces.

1 Heat ½ cup (125 ml) of the coconut milk in a small saucepan over medium-high heat. Cook, stirring constantly, until it reduces by about half and thickens considerably (about 5 minutes). Mix in the curry paste and cook for an additional minute.
2 Pour in the remaining coconut milk and the stock, then add the cinnamon, ginger, sugar, fish sauce, and tamarind. Bring to a boil.
3 Stir in the onions, potatoes and peanuts, and cook for 5 minutes, then stir in the oyster mushrooms and simmer until the potatoes are just cooked through.
4 Taste the sauce and adjust the seasoning using fish sauce, salt and/or sugar.

**Serves 4–6   Preparation time: 10 mins
Cooking time: 15 mins**

2 tablespoons oil

¼ cup (70 g) green curry paste

4 cups (1 liter) vegetable, chicken or pork stock/
broth

1 tablespoon Thai palm sugar or light brown sugar

1 tablespoon fish sauce or soy sauce

3 stalks lemongrass, tender inner part of bottom
third only, bruised

6 slices galangal (substitute ginger)

6 kaffir lime leaves (substitute 1 teaspoon grated
lime zest)

4 cups (50–100 g per cup) vegetables—cut into
bite-sized slices, pieces or strips
  • Long Cooking (5 minutes)—Eggplant, long
  beans, onions, carrots
  • Quick Cooking (3 minutes)—Mushrooms, chilies, bell peppers, beans, peas, asparagus, green
  papaya
  • Instant Cooking (just stir in)—Asian greens
  (choy sum, bok choy…), snow peas, cooked
  bamboo shoots

1 tablespoon green peppercorns (optional)

¼ cup (7 g) Thai basil leaves

1 red finger-length chili, sliced into thin rings or
slivers

1 Heat the oil and curry paste in a medium saucepan over medium-high heat and cook for 1 minute.

2 Pour in the stock, sugar, fish sauce, lemongrass, galangal, kaffir lime leaves, and bring to a boil. Lower the heat to simmer for 3–5 minutes. Add the vegetables in stages according to their cook time.

3 Taste the sauce and adjust seasoning with fish sauce, salt and/or sugar. Stir in the green peppercorns (if using) and basil leaves.

4 Remove from the heat, transfer into a serving bowl and garnish with sliced chilies.

Mixed Vegetable Jungle Curry

A seasonal bounty of vegetables shine in this northern Thai-style jungle curry that doesn't include coconut milk. When available I use krachai, a rhizome in the same family as galangal, it's difficult to find fresh outside of Thailand—the frozen variety can work. I have outlined the vegetables in categories based on cooking time, if there are others you would like to include just try to add them into one of these categories and cook accordingly. Remember to tell your guests that the whole aromatics (lemongrass, kaffir lime leaves, and galangal) are not meant to be eaten, or you may opt to simply take them out before serving.

Chapter Six

Noodles and Rice

The history of rice goes back more than 4000 years in Thailand when they began to cultivate this staple grain, it's possible that it was in Thailand that people first started to cultivate rice.

Although it seems like every Thai restaurant serves steamed Jasmine Rice (page 102), this is not true. Technically it's not steamed, it's cooked submerged in water until it absorbs the water, yielding a steaming pot or aromatic, it's what Thais call "Thai Ho Mali Rice."

When I want a bit more excitement, I cook up a batch of Pineapple Fried Jasmine Rice (page 103), fried rice is actually my favorite breakfast food, I usually use leftover rice, once chilled it separates easily into individual grains. Instead of scrambling the eggs I sometimes like to fry an egg sunny-side up and top the mound of rice with it, whooah, get ready for a great way to start the day. Regardless of how it's served, I cannot go a few days without some plain white rice. Its sweet aroma, savory taste, and shear simplicity is one of life's great pleasures. When I don't have some for a while, I begin to crave its taste and when I have broken my fast I savor that first bite.

Are you a big shot, or what Thais call a *sen yai* or "big noodle." This expression demonstrates how important noodles are in the Thai culture. Many people are surprised to see how many dry noodles are used in Thai food, they are so convenient to keep on hand and when you need some noodles you can soak them while you get everything else ready. They can be stir-fried without ever boiling them, that's what you do for the Tamarind Noodles with Chicken, Pork or Shrimp (page 94) that were inspired by Pad Thai noodles. You also have the option of cooking them first for 2 minutes in boiling water, leeching out some of the starch, this is done with the Rice Ribbon Noodles with Basil (page 96).

Thais invent food every day, one recent addition to the Thai repertoire is instant Japanese ramen noodles. Street food vendors keep the packs of noodles on the shelves for those that have become addicted to these wheat based, fried until dry, noodle nests (that's why they cook so quickly). I have re-created the Bangkok "Night Market" Ramen (page 100) so you can try this at home.

Tamarind Noodles with Chicken, Pork, or Shrimp

I always keep some dried rice noodles in the house for when I am in the mood for easy recipes like this one! The flavor profile is similar to the infamous Pad Thai, this may have a long list of ingredients but use what you have on hand, these are just guidelines, especially with the protein and vegetables. You can be flexible and creative, starting with the Peanut Tamarind Sauce and adjusting seasoning to your tastes as you go.

Serves 4–6
Preparation time: 5 mins + soaking time
Cooking time: 10 mins

½ lb (250 g) chicken, pork or shrimp—cut into bite-sized pieces strips
1 tablespoon Thai palm sugar or light brown sugar
1 tablespoon fish sauce
½ lb (250 g) dried flat rice noodles (about ¼ inch/6 mm wide)
2 tablespoons oil
¼ cup (25 g) thinly sliced shallots
2 tablespoons minced garlic
2 cups (120 g) Asian greens (choy sum or bok choy), bite-sized pieces
¼ cup (7 g) chopped coriander leaves (cilantro)
1 cup (50 g) bean sprouts
¼ cup (30 g) chopped roasted or deep-fried peanuts
1 lime, cut into wedges

PEANUT TAMARIND SAUCE
2 tablespoons Sriracha Chili Sauce (page 35)
2 tablespoons Thai palm sugar or light brown sugar
2 tablespoons fish sauce
3 tablespoons Tamarind Pulp or concentrate (page 25)

¼ cup (65 ml) water
½ cup (75 g) chopped roasted or deep-fried peanuts

1 Marinate the chicken, pork or shrimp in the palm sugar and fish sauce for at least half an hour.
2 Cover the rice noodles in room temperature water and soak for 30 minutes, drain and set aside.
3 Make the Peanut Tamarind Sauce by whisking all the ingredients together in a small bowl, set aside.
4 Heat a large skillet or wok over high heat. Swirl the oil in the skillet to coat the entire surface, and keep heating the skillet until it is very hot and the oil begins to smoke.

5 Stir-fry the shallots and garlic until aromatic, about 20 seconds. Add the chicken, pork or shrimp and cook until about 50% cooked, add the noodles and stir-fry until they begin to soften and brown on some edges.
6 Mix in the Asian greens and Peanut Tamarind Sauce until the noodles are coated well, then stir in the coriander leaves and bean sprouts.
7 Remove from the heat, taste and adjust the seasoning with fish sauce, tamarind, and Sriracha Chili Sauce.
8 Pile the noodles high on a plate, sprinkle with the peanuts and garnish with lime wedges to squeeze on the noodles right before you devour them.

1 Soak the rice noodles for 30 minutes.

2 Mix in the Asian greens and Peanut Tamarind Sauce until the noodles are well coated.

Rice Ribbon Noodles with Basil

This noodle recipe gives us another use for the versatile roasted chili paste in soya bean oil, affectionately called Thai Chili Jam. You can buy it ready to use or make your own (page 36). I soak and cook the noodles since I want the noodles to stay saucy, different than the drier and chewy noodle recipes, like the Tamarind Noodles with Chicken, Pork, or Shrimp (page 94). The chili sauce is misleadingly red and not as spicy as it may look, since I like the burn, when I make this I add a few minced Thai chilies.

Serves 4
Preparation time: 5 mins + soaking time
Cooking time: 10 mins

½ lb (250 g) dried flat rice noodles (about ¼ in/6 mm wide)

4 cups (1 liter) water

2 tablespoons oil

2 teaspoons minced garlic

2 tablespoons chili paste in soya bean oil (*nahm prik pow*)

1 cup (6 oz/175 g) ground pork or chicken

1 cup (250 ml) chicken, pork or vegetable stock/broth

1 tablespoon Thai palm sugar or light brown sugar

2 tablespoons fish sauce

¼ teaspoon ground white pepper

2 tablespoons minced coriander stems (cilantro stems)

¼ cup (7 g) Thai basil leaves

½ cup (10 g) mint leaves

1 Soak the noodles in room temperature water for 30 minutes. Drain well. Bring the water to a rolling boil, stir the noodles into the water and cooked for 1–2 minutes or until just cooked through, Immediately drain and rinse with cool water until it's cool to the touch. Drain well and set aside.

2 Heat a large skillet or wok over high heat. Swirl the oil in the skillet to coat the entire surface, stir in the garlic and chili paste, then stir in the pork or chicken and continue to stir-fry, breaking it up as needed until it is almost cooked. Stir in the stock/broth, sugar, fish sauce, pepper, and coriander stems. Bring the mixture to a boil, then stir in the noodles and cook, mixing constantly until the noodles softens and absorbs most of the liquid, making them slightly saucy.

3 Remove from the heat, stir in the Thai basil leaves and mint leaves until they just wilt. Taste and adjust seasoning with fish sauce, palm sugar, and/or salt.

Rice Ribbon Noodles with Basil

Garlic Soy Noodles with Pork

The textural contrast of crispy pan-fried noodles with a silky center makes me smile! This recipe shows how stir-frying in stages can create a superior textural flavor experience. If you can't get the wide fresh rice noodles, then you can soak dried noodles in room temperature water for 30 minutes, drop them into boiling water for a quick 1–2 minute cook time, drain and rinse with cool water, drain again and toss with a touch of oil.

Serves 4
Preparation time: 5 mins + marinating time
Cooking time: 10 mins

12 oz (350 g) boneless pork leg, shoulder (butt), or loin, cut into bite-sized pieces
1 tablespoon sweet soy sauce
4 tablespoons oil (divided use)
½ cup (125 ml) chicken, pork or vegetable stock/broth
2 tablespoons soy sauce
1 teaspoon Thai palm sugar or light brown sugar
1 teaspoon sesame oil
¼ teaspoon ground white pepper
1 teaspoon cornstarch
1 lb (500 g) fresh flat rice noodles (substitute 8 oz/250 g cooked dried noodles tossed with 1 teaspoon oil)
2 cups (160 g) Chinese broccoli, cut into bite-sized pieces
¼ cup (35 g) thinly evenly sliced garlic
1 cup (80 g) green onions (scallions), bite-sized pieces
2–4 red finger-length chilies, sliced thinly
¼ cup (7 g) Thai basil leaves

1 Marinate the pork in the sweet soy sauce and 1 tablespoon of the oil for at least 30 minutes.
2 Whisk the stock/broth, soy sauce, sugar, sesame oil, pepper, and cornstarch together in a small bowl to create the seasoning sauce, set aside.
3 Get organized to stir-fry by organizing all the items in the order that they will go in the skillet, this allows you to add things quickly!
4 Heat a large skillet or wok over high heat. Swirl the second tablespoon of oil in the skillet to coat the entire surface, and keep heating the skillet until it is very hot and the oil begins to smoke. Distribute the noodles in the skillet and do not stir, allow them to brown first then stir gently and allow more of them to brown, continue this until you have a desirable brown color on the edges of the noodles. Transfer the noodles to a serving platter and keep warm by covering it loosely.
5 Wipe out the same skillet to remove any brown bits or stuck noodles, then swirl the third tablespoon of oil in the skillet to coat the entire surface, and keep heating the skillet until it is very hot and the oil begins to smoke. Stir-fry the pork and broccoli until cooked through, arrange on top of the noodles, keep warm.
6 Heat the last tablespoon of oil with the garlic over medium heat and cook until aromatic and just beginning to brown. Re-whisk and stir in the premixed sauce, bring to a boil. Add the green onions and chilies then taste and adjust seasoning with soy sauce and sugar. Stir in the basil until it wilts.
7 Evenly pour the sauce over the meat, greens, and noodles.

Green Papaya Salad Noodle Bowl

Bright flavors and a textural explosion are trademarks of the Northeastern som tum salad. This version I discovered wandering the rural roads of the southern island of Koh Samui in search of food. I listened for the thumping sound from large wooden pestles, they use these in massive mortars especially formed for papaya salad. Scooting along on a motorbike we discovered a mobile street food master crafting a papaya salad served on *khanom jin*, the slightly fermented rice noodles. We ducked out of the scorching sun under a tree and feasted on the spicy-sweet-and-sour salad, it was truly a life changing experience. This recipe pays homage to that flavorful hot afternoon.

Serves 4–6
Preparation time: 10 mins + soaking and marinating times
Cooking time: 5 mins

¾ lb (350 g) dried rice vermicelli noodles
4 cups (1 liter) water
2 cups (200 g) green papaya, peeled and sliced into very thin strips
1 cup (100 g) long beans or green beans, cut into bite-sized pieces
1 cup (75 g) shaved green cabbage
1 cup (150 g) halved cherry or grape tomatoes
8 oz (250 g) poached or grilled shrimp, peeled
½ cup (75 g) chopped roasted or deep-fried peanuts

DRESSING
2 teaspoons minced garlic
1 shallot, chopped
2–4 Thai chilies
1 tablespoon yellow, red or green curry paste
¼ cup (75 g) Thai palm sugar or light brown sugar
¼ cup (65 ml) fish sauce
¼ cup (65 ml) fresh lime juice
¼ cup (65 ml) water
½ teaspoon sea salt or kosher salt

1 Soak the noodles in room temperature water for 30 minutes. Drain well. Bring the water to a roaring boil, stir the noodles into the water and cooked for 1-2 minutes or until just cooked through. Immediately drain and rinse with cool water until cool to the touch. Divide the noodles into a neat nest between 4–6 shallow bowls. Cover and keep at room temperature.

2 Make the Dressing by grinding the garlic, shallot, and chilies into a coarse paste in a mortar or mini food processor. Add the curry paste, palm sugar, fish sauce, lime juice, water and salt, and mix until the palm sugar is dissolved. Set aside.
3 Mix the papaya, long beans, and cabbage in a separate large bowl. Use your hands to massage the mixture firmly, softening the vegetables so they can absorb more dressing. Mix in the Dressing, tomatoes and shrimp. Let marinate for 5 minutes. Taste and adjust seasoning with fish sauce, sugar and/or salt.
4 Divide the dressed salad evenly on top of the noodles, sprinkle with peanuts.

1 Cut the green papaya into very thin strips.

2 Divide the noodles between 4–6 bowls..

3 Divide the dressed salad evenly on top of the noodles.

Bangkok "Night Market" Ramen

Ramen noodles originated in China, Japan popularized them, and street vendors in Thailand's bustling city of Bangkok also sell them. Fresh ramen noodles are becoming more available in western markets but they're still not easy to find, so I use of the dried ramen noodles here. These blocks of noodles are typically fried as part of the drying process and this makes them cook "instantly." The ramen dishes found late at night on the streets of Bangkok are offered with a choice of various meats or seafood.

Serves 4   Preparation time: 10 mins
Cooking time: 10 mins

9 cups (2 liters) water
3 packages of instant ramen noodles (about 2 oz/60 g per package)
1 tablespoons minced garlic
1 tablespoon minced ginger
1 tablespoons minced coriander stems (cilantro stems)
¼ cup (20 g) chopped green onions (scallions)
2 tablespoons chicken, pork or vegetable stock/broth
2 tablespoons soy sauce
1 tablespoon oyster sauce
1–2 tablespoons Sriracha Chili Sauce (page 35)
2 tablespoons oil
½ lb (250 g) chicken, beef or pork, thinly sliced
2 cups (120 g) Asian greens (water spinach, choy sum, or bok choy), sliced into small pieces
¼ cup (40 g) shredded or matchstick strip carrots
⅛ teaspoon ground white pepper
¼ cup (7 g) Thai basil leaves

1 Boil the water in a medium saucepan, add the ramen noodles (save the seasoning packets for another use). Stir well and cook for 2 minutes, drain, rinse with water until cool, drain very well and set aside.

2 Take a moment to get ready to stir-fry. Combine the garlic, ginger, coriander stems, and green onions. In a separate small bowl, whisk the stock/broth, soy sauce, oyster sauce, and Sriracha Chili Sauce together.

3 Heat a large skillet or wok over high heat. Swirl then oil in the skillet to coat the entire surface, and keep heating the skillet until it is very hot and the oil begins to smoke.

4 Stir in the garlic mixture and cook until aromatic, about 15 seconds. Stir in the meat and stir-fry until about half cooked.

5 Mix in the noodles and stir-fry, only stirring occasionally so the noodles brown in some parts (sometimes I drizzle a bit of oil to facilitate this). Since the noodles are already cooked you only need to stir-fry for a minute or two. Mix in the greens and carrots.

6 Pour in the sauce mixture and cook until you are able to mix all the ingredients evenly. Stir in the basil leaves until just wilted. Taste and adjust seasoning with soy sauce, Sriracha Chili Sauce and a touch of sugar if needed.

Cinnamon-scented Beef Noodle Soup

Each trip I take down Thailand's Chao Praya River, I am compelled to try to locate Thai boat noodles, like aromatic sirens they call out to me with their intoxicating fragrance. This simplified version uses a premade stock to save hours of simmering meaty bones. A quick infusion of caramelized onions and sweet spices stirs up memories of the floating markets with the sun rising behind the thousands of Thai temples. Like most cooks in Asia, I use all of the fresh coriander (cilantro) by using the stems in the broth and using the leaves for the garnish.

Makes 4 full meal noodle bowls or 6 servings as part of multi-course meal
Preparation time: 10 mins   Cooking time: 20 mins

9 cups (2 liters) water
½ lb (250 g) dried flat rice noodles (about ¼ inch/6 mm wide), soaked in water for 30 mins
½ lb (250 g) beef (flank, strip loin, round or sirloin), thinly sliced so it will cook
3 cups (180 g) Asian greens (water spinach, choy sum, or bok choy), sliced into small pieces
1 cup (80 g) green onions (scallions), sliced into lengths
¼ cup (10 g) coriander leaves (cilantro)
1 tablespoon Fried Garlic (page 37)
1 lime, cut into wedges

SCENTED BROTH
1 tablespoon oil
2 cups (270 g) onions, sliced
6 pieces star anise
2 sticks cinnamon, about 3 inch (7.5 cm) long
2 stalks lemongrass, tender inner part of bottom third only, smashed
2 tablespoons chili paste in soya bean oil (*nahm prik pow*)

9 cups (2 liters) store-bought or homemade beef stock/broth
¼ cup (15 g) roughly chopped coriander stems (cilantro stems)

1 Prepare the Scented Broth by heating the oil in a large saucepan over high heat, add the onions, star anise, cinnamon, and lemongrass. Cook, stirring occasionally until the onions turn golden brown, about 3–5 minutes. Add the chili paste, stock/broth, and coriander stems, bring to a boil and simmer for 10 minutes. Strain through a wire mesh strainer. Pour the strained broth back into the pot, taste and adjust the seasoning with salt. Keep hot over a low heat.
2 Boil the water over high heat, cook the rice noodles until cooked through (about 1-2 minutes), drain and divide evenly among large serving bowls. Divide the beef among the bowls on one side of noodles.
3 Stir the greens and green onions into the Scented Broth and cook for 30 seconds. Ladle the hot broth over the beef to cook it as you fill the bowls. Sprinkle with coriander leaves and Fried Garlic. Serve with lime wedges and provide everyone with a large spoon and chopsticks.

Cinnamon-scented Beef Noodle Soup

Steamed Sticky Rice and Jasmine Rice

Jasmine Rice

Jasmine rice is so easy to cook, especially if you have a rice cooker! Thai jasmine rice is special, so much so that the Thai government has secured the name Thai Ho Mali rice to preserve it's distinction from others. Jasmine rice has a naturally occurring aromatic compound called 2-Acetyl-1-pyrroline, now don't be scared, it's also present in other favorites like popcorn, and pandanus leaves.

Steamed Sticky Rice

Delightfully chewy, the northern Thais use this to scoop up fiery papaya salads, spice enriched curries and to make sticky rice with mangos. Soaking the rice overnight gives the best results but a short bath in the tepid water will suffice. I use a traditional cone-like bamboo steamer in my kitchen, but any tight lidded steamer will do. Use your thumb and two fingers to gently knead the cooked rice, then it can be used efficiently to scoop up saucy salads and curries.

Serves 4–6   Preparation time: 5 mins
Cooking time: 30–45 mins

2 cups (450 g) uncooked long grain sticky rice (glutinous rice)

1 Generously cover the sticky rice with room temperature water and soak at room temperature overnight or in lukewarm water (100°F/40°C) for 1 hour, drain well.
2 Transfer the drained rice to a steamer and if need be, line the steamer with cheesecloth to prevent the rice from falling through. Cover and steam over high heat with copious amounts of water boiling for 30 to 45 minutes until cooked through.

Serves 4–6
Preparation time: 5 mins
Cooking time: 30 minutes plus resting time (if not using a rice cooker)

2 cups (450 g) uncooked jasmine rice
2½ cups (625 ml) water

1 Place the rice in a strainer, rinse until almost clear—about 30 seconds.
2 Transfer to the rice cooker and add the water, press the button and you're done. If you don't have a rice cooker, grab a small saucepan with a tight fitting lid. Combine the rice and measured water (plus two more tablespoons water), bring to a boil over medium heat. Once boiling, cover and lower the heat to lowest setting and simmer for 20 minutes. Remove from the heat and rest (DO NOT OPEN) for 10 minutes.
3 Gently fluff the rice and serve.

Pineapple Fried Jasmine Rice

Leftover rice never tasted so good! Rice that has been cooked and chilled works better for this dish since the grains stay separated more easily. For a dramatic presentation some people like to serve the rice in a halved pineapple. Towards the end, stir in ½ lb (250 g) of crabmeat or cooked shrimp for seafood fried rice. Most Thai cooks would season the fried rice with shrimp or crab paste that come in small jars, labeled as Shrimp or Crab in Soya Bean oil, since it's hard to find in some areas I have used the chili paste that is used in many other recipes in this book (see page 13).

Serves 4–6   Preparation time: 10 mins   Cooking time: 15 mins

2 tablespoons oil (divided use)
1 egg, lightly beaten
½ cup (50 g) diced red onion
1 tablespoon minced ginger
1 tablespoon minced garlic
4 cups (800 g) cooked or leftover Jasmine Rice (page 102), grains separated
2 tablespoons chili paste in soya bean oil (*nahm prik pow*)
1 tablespoon fish sauce
¼ teaspoon ground white pepper
¼ teaspoon sea salt or kosher salt
1 cup (225 g) diced pineapple, fresh or canned, (if canned, drain well before using)
½ cup (20 g) roughly chopped coriander leaves (cilantro)
½ cup (75 g) toasted cashews, roughly chopped
2 limes cut into wedges, to garnish
1 cucumber, peeled, thinly sliced diagonally, to garnish
6 coriander (cilantro) sprigs, to garnish

1 Heat 1 tablespoon of the oil in a large non-stick skillet or wok over highest heat until it begins to smoke. Pour the egg into the skillet and tilt to make a thin layer. Cook until semi-set, then scramble the eggs until lightly browned and broken up. Remove the eggs from the skillet and set aside.
2 Coat the same skillet with the remaining tablespoon of oil and stir-fry the onion, ginger, and garlic for about 30 seconds—until the onions become translucent and the garlic just begins to brown.
3 Stir in the rice, chili paste, fish sauce, pepper and salt. Mix to coat the rice with all the ingredients, then stop stirring and let it cook for 15-second increments, to achieve some brown bits. Continue this process for about 3–5 minutes until the rice is nicely browned.
4 Add the cooked egg and diced pineapple and cook for about a minute to heat the pineapple. Stir in the chopped coriander leaves.
5 Transfer to a platter, sprinkle the cashews on top and garnish with the lime, cucumber, and coriander sprigs.

Chapter Seven

Desserts and Drinks

The Thais love sweets. Known as *khanom*, they are usually eaten as a snack, although in fine dining restaurants they may be served as a final course to a meal. A simple sweet that highlights the fruit is the Fresh Mangos in Sweet Coconut Cream with Roasted Peanuts (page 112). Eating fruit at various stages of ripeness (great way to use under-ripe fruit) with a chili infused salt is something you must taste. Try the recipe for Fresh Sweet Pineapple with Chili Salt (page 109), once you try it you will definitely begin to experiment!

Thailand's climate is usually hot and so the Thais drink a great deal of liquid. What they might traditionally drink with a meal and what they drink at other times is very different. There is a great sensibility to this. Why would they want to contaminate the pure flavors of a lime leaf fragranced green curry with a soda?

Water, weak tea, or even soups are very common drinks. Weak tea is created to show that the water has been boiled (to sterilize it), technically the water in Thailand is potable (I drink it, although I get surprised looks when I do), so pitchers of this tinted tea sits on tables for those to help themselves to before, during, or after a meal, not infecting the delicate balance of flavor. This is where soup steps in as one of the most logical component to act as a beverage.

Most meals are comprised of several dishes, and one of those is a mildly seasoned broth based soup. This soup is great for cleansing the palate, allowing you to savor the nuances of each recipe as you consume various dishes.

Between meals, I sustain my energy with the local jet-fuel, comprised of strong brews of coffee or tea subdued by condensed or evaporated milk creating the Thai Iced Coffee (page 114) and Thai Iced Tea (page 114) that have become favorites to most "farang," western foreigners. I also like the lighter Lemongrass Iced Tea (page 115), not only refreshing, but a great way to use up your lemongrass tops leftover from other recipes. Fresh fruit juices and modern day sodas are also common place on street carts and restaurants around Thailand, the energy giving Red Bull energy drink was actually invented in Thailand. Creating cocktails is fun and I have included one recipe for you to sample, the Spiced Mango Cocktail (page 113), which combines fresh basil, limes, chilies, ginger ale, and vodka into one slamming drink.

Grilled Pineapple with Caramel Sauce

Slightly charred slices of ripe pineapple drizzled with caramel sauce are a decadent treat. Not a traditional Thai recipe since Thais generally eat fruit without many enhancements, nevertheless a recipe your friends and family will love. I have found that the coconut caramel sauce is great to have in my refrigerator for spooning onto ice cream, drizzling over a warm bread pudding, or even a few spoons stirred into my morning coffee … really!

Serves 6–8
Preparation time: 10 mins
Cooking time: 20 mins

1 ripe pineapple
1 tablespoon melted unsalted butter
¼ cup (20 g) toasted shredded un-
    sweetened coconut

CARAMEL SAUCE
1 cup (200 g) sugar
¼ cup (65 ml) water
¾ cup (180 ml) coconut milk
¼ teaspoon sea salt or kosher salt
4 pandanus leaves

1 Prepare the Caramel Sauce by combining the sugar and water in a medium saucepan, cover and bring to a boil over high heat. Do not stir. Uncover and boil for about 5 minutes, long enough to achieve a dark amber syrup. The sugar will be at 360°F/182°C. Remove from the heat and slowly whisk in the coconut milk. The mixture will boil rapidly and will give off a lot of steam—be careful!! Stir in the salt and pandanus leaves, let it steep until room temperature. Remove the pandanus leaves, squeezing out all the liquid into the sauce. Discard the leaves. This sauce can be stored at room temperature for a few days, otherwise refrigerate for a month.
2 Peel the pineapple, cut in half lengthwise, then cut the halves in half exposing the core. Make a cut lengthwise to remove the core, leaving you with four quarters of the pineapple. Brush both sides of each slice very lightly with the butter.

3 Preheat grill, clean well, wipe with a cloth towel. Grill the pineapple wedges for no more than 2 minutes on flat sides only, you are really just trying to infuse the flavor and not cook them too much. If they are slow to brown only cook one side and serve them that side up for presentation.
4 Slice across the narrow diameter into ½-inch (1.25 cm) thick slices then arrange the pineapple on plates or a platter, drizzle with ¼ of the Caramel Sauce (serve the rest on the side). Sprinkle with the toasted coconut before serving.

Grilled Bananas with Sesame Seeds

Simply delicious, grilled baby bananas are a typical street food in Thailand. Long rows of these miniature fruits lay above smoldering charcoals, absorbing the smoky aroma. I transform this into a more complete dessert by drizzling them with rich condensed milk, toss on a few sesame seeds, and a final negligible pinch of salt balances the sweetness.

Serves 4–6
Preparation time: 5 mins
Cooking time: 20 mins

8–12 small ripe "finger" bananas
¼ cup (65 ml) sweetened condensed milk
1 tablespoon toasted sesame seeds
Pinch of sea salt or kosher salt

1 Rinse the bananas, do not peel. Preheat a grill over medium heat. Distribute the bananas on the grill and cook, rotating often for about 10–20 minutes depending on variety and ripeness.
2 Remove to a serving platter, rest for 3 minutes to cool down slightly, then carefully make an incision along the top of each banana allowing you to pull back the skin to expose the now roasted sweet banana.
3 Serve warm, drizzled with condensed milk, and a sprinkle of sesame seeds and touch of salt.

1 Grill the bananas for about 10–20 minutes, depending on variety and ripeness.

2 Make an incision along the top of each banana. Pull back the skin to expose the flesh.

Fresh Sweet Pineapple with Chili Salt

Yes, chili and fruit. It's common all across Southeast Asia and once you taste it you will understand why it's so popular of a flavor experience. I must admit, even the best chef cannot create flavor profiles as amazing as those naturally found in nature—especially fruit. That's why just a touch of spicy salt is all some fruit needs to balance the inherently sweet taste. I have even added some kaffir lime leaves (or lime zest) to the salt mixture. Once you have some of this chili salt on hand you will find many uses—some traditionally Asian like grilled seafood dipped in it (I like to squeeze a bit of lime first) and some more contemporary uses like on popcorn, French fries, or the even the rim of a cocktail.

Serves 4–6
Preparation time: 10 mins

2–4 Thai chilies, preferably red
2 tablespoons sea salt or kosher
    salt
2 teaspoons sugar
Platter of Assorted Fruit: pineapple,
    mangos, pomelo segments, green
    guavas, or green apples

1 Grind the chilies, salt and sugar in a mortar or mini-food processor until the chilies are finely ground. If the mixture becomes wet (some chilies are very moist), spread them out and bake at 250°F (115°C) for about ½ hour until dried, then grind in dried mortar or processor again.
2 Serve a small bowl of the chili-salt with the fruit, each person dips to their liking.

Jasmine Rice Pudding

Rice pudding, the world's favorite comfort food gets a Thai infusion in this recipe with the intoxicating pandanus herb. These slender leaves infuse their subtle aroma to this after dinner dish. Since most people are used to traditional rice pudding with dried fruits and nuts, go ahead and be creative. For me, if anything, I like some fresh mangos, pineapple, or lychees. The crowning glory of roasted cashews or toasted shredded coconut add a crunchy roasted flavor.

Serves 4–6
Preparation time: 5 mins
Cooking time: 40 mins

1 cup (225 g) uncooked jasmine rice
3½ cups (850 ml) milk
4 cups (1 liter) coconut milk (divided use)
1 cup (200 g) sugar
1 teaspoon sea salt or kosher salt
6 pandanus leaves
½ cup (75 g) toasted cashews and/or coconut

1 Place the rice in a strainer, rinse until almost clear—about 30 seconds.
2 Stir the milk, 3 cups (750 ml) of the coconut milk, the sugar and salt together in a medium saucepan. Bring to a boil.
3 Stir in the rice and bring the mixture back to a boil. Lower the heat to low-medium and gently simmer for about 30 minutes until the rice is cook, stirring often to prevent scorching at the bottom. Stir in the remaining coconut milk and pandanus leaves, let it steep until room temperature. Remove the pandanus leaves, squeezing out all the liquid into the sauce. Discard the leaves.
4 Spoon the pudding into serving bowls and chill in the refrigerator until ready to serve. Top with the toasted nuts and/or coconut before serving.

Coconut Pudding with Seasonal Fruit

These boil and chill puddings are a snap to make ahead of time. Small, pan fried, or steamed coconut custards are found in Thailand, but to make this simpler version I recalled my time cooking in Hawaii. I was always fond of simple Haupia, their coconut sweet snack, that they make very firm and cut into pieces. This recipe creates a spoonable custard so I leave it in the small bowl and top it with seasonal fruit—diced tropical fruits like pineapple, mango, and banana are guaranteed winners, but don't hesitate to try other fruits like ripe kiwis, peaches, or plums. Try it with the Caramel Sauce (page 106).

Serves 4–6
Preparation time: 5 mins
Cooking time: 15 mins + chilling time

2 cups (500 ml) coconut milk
¾ cup (180 ml) water
6 tablespoons sugar
¼ cup (35 g) cornstarch
1 cup (225 g) diced seasonal fruit (pineapple, mango, bananas etc)

1 Whisk the coconut milk, water, sugar, and cornstarch together in a small saucepan until smooth. Heat over medium-high heat while gently whisking constantly until the mixture comes to a full boil. Remove from the heat, spoon/pour into small bowls, cool to room temperature then cover with plastic wrap and chill overnight.
2 Serve with a topping or side bowl of diced seasonal fruit.

Fresh Mangos in Sweet Coconut Cream with Roasted Peanuts

Mangos and sticky rice is a favorite, this simplified version (no rice) focuses on the best mangos you can find. Other ripe fruits, like pineapple or bananas (which I dust with sugar and torch to caramelize), can be used or even some non-conventional fruit, such as peaches, pair well with the coconut. Traditionally toasted and soaked dried mung beans are used for a crunchy garnish. This recipe uses peanuts, or you could use toasted sesame seeds. For a better sensory experience I will pound a mixture of pan-roasted sesame, coconut and peanuts, and season with chili flakes, sugar, and salt, and use this as a final topping.

Serves 4–6
Preparation time: 10 mins
Cooking time: 15 mins

1 cup (250 ml) coconut milk (divided use)
1 teaspoon cornstarch
2 tablespoons Thai palm sugar or light
   brown sugar
¼ teaspoon sea salt or kosher salt
4 pandanus leaves (optional)
4 ripe mangos—chilled well
¼ cup (30 g) chopped roasted or deep-
   fried peanuts

1 Whisk ¼ cup (65 ml) of the coconut milk with the cornstarch together in a small bowl. Combine the remaining coconut milk, sugar, salt, and pandanus leaf in a small saucepan and bring to a boil over a low heat. Remove from the heat to steep for 5 minutes. Remove the pandanus leaves, squeezing out all liquid possible to maximize flavor extraction. Discard the leaves. Slowly drizzle in the coconut cornstarch mixture while whisking constantly, bring to a boil, the sauce will thicken considerably. Remove from the heat and cool to room temperature.
2 Peel the mangos, cut two large "cheeks" from each side of the mango seed. Trim the remaining flesh from the seed (you can snack on those tidbits). Slice each slab of mango into thick slices. Arrange decoratively on a plate, spoon the coconut mixture on top of the mangos and sprinkle with the peanuts.

Spiced Mango Cocktail

Spiced Mango Cocktail

This rockin' cocktail burns with the sweet heat of mango and chilies. Thai basil's anise-like aroma punctuates the cocktail and ginger ale giving it an effervescent sparkle that can be gulped down faster than you realize...proceed carefully as you enter the tropical mango cocktail zone!

Serves 4
Preparation time: 10 mins

2 cups (370 g) ripe mangos, peeled and pitted
¼ cup (7 g) Thai basil leaves
6 kaffir lime leaves or 1 teaspoon lime zest
2 tablespoons Thai palm sugar or light brown sugar
8 fl oz (250 ml) brandy, vodka or rum
2 cups (500 ml) ginger ale
4 cups (500 g) ice cubes
1 lime, cut into 8 wedges
4 Thai chilies, split lengthwise from the point, leaving the stem intact
4 small sprigs of Thai basil

1 Make a fine purée of the mango, basil, lime leaves, sugar, and brandy in a blender. Strain through a wire mesh strainer, then stir in the ginger ale.
2 Fill four 8 oz (250 ml) glasses with the ice cubes.
3 Divide the mango purée into the glasses. Squeeze two lime wedges into each glass, then add the squeezed lime wedges to the glasses.
4 Garnish each glasses with the Thai chilies on the rim and put a basil sprig in the drink.

Thai Iced Coffee

This fabulously strong brew's bitterness is calmed with sweetened condensed milk and will keep you going on those hot summer days when you need a lift. Make sure to avoid cans of sweetened condensed filled milk where manufacturers have added oil and other useless ingredients. Roasted sesame seeds, soy beans, and corn enrich Thai coffee mixtures and hence this bold concoction is labeled as Oliang Powder/Mixture. Thai coffee is readily available online or at local Asian markets.

Serves 4–6
Preparation time: 5 mins
Cooking time: 10 mins

1¼ cups (155 g) Thai coffee mixture "Oliang Powder"
4 cups (1 liter) water
1 can (14 oz/414 ml) sweetened condensed milk
6–8 cups (750 g–1 kg) crushed ice
4–6 straws

1 Measure the coffee into the filter of the electric coffee maker. Fill the machine with water and run according to manufacture's instructions. You may also use a French press to make this coffee base.
2 Stir the condensed milk into the brewed coffee. Chill in the refrigerator.
3 Fill the glasses with crushed ice, then top with the chilled coffee, it's best if served with straws.

> **Stove top method:** Stir the coffee grounds into the boiling water. Brew for 5 minutes. Strain through a coffee filter, very fine wire mesh strainer or cheesecloth.
> **Hot Thai coffee method:** Fill each cup with 3 to 4 tablespoons of condensed milk; top with 1 cup (250 ml) of hot coffee.

Thai Iced Tea

Thai tea in restaurants is often too sweet, so here you have the opportunity to make your own at home. One day I had lunch with my friend, Khun Charinee, formerly from the Tourism Authority of Thailand and she revealed a non-dairy version of Thai tea with wedges of limes, it was utterly refreshing. I have even experimented with using coconut milk, non-traditional but still delicious. The bright orange color was originally created with the addition of ground tamarind seeds, sadly replaced with artificial colors.

Serves 4–6
Preparation time: 5 mins
Cooking time: 10 mins

4 cups (1.75 liter) water
½ cup (300 g) sugar
1 cup (175 g) Thai tea mixture
1 cups (500 ml) evaporated milk or water
6–8 cups (750 g–1 kg) crushed ice
1 lime, cut into wedges
4–6 straws

1 Combine the water and sugar in a saucepan, and bring to a boil over high heat. Remove from the heat and whisk in the tea mixture. Steep for 5 minutes, then strain through a coffee filter or fine wire mesh strainer. Chill the tea mixture in the refrigerator.
2 Fill the glasses with the crushed ice, then top up with the chilled tea.
3 Choose which style of tea you want:
Option 1—Drizzle with ½ cup (125 ml) evaporated milk into the tea. Serve with straw.
Option 2—Squeeze a lime wedge in each glass, then fill with ½ cup (125 ml) water. Give a stir and serve with straw.

Thai Iced Tea with Lime

Lemongrass Iced Tea

Thai Iced Coffee

Lemongrass Iced Tea

Citrus aromas fill the kitchen as you quickly craft this refreshing iced tea from slender aromatic stalks of lemongrass. You can even use leftover tops that you have stashed away in the freezer. Sometimes (well, often) I am in the mood for a cocktail and then I add a splash or vodka, squeeze in a couple of lime wedges and a splash of soda water for a lively lemongrass tea cocktail. Add some mint leaves and it beats any mojito you've ever had.

Serves 4–6
Preparation time: 5 mins
Cooking time: 20 mins

8 whole stalks of lemongrass (or 16 lemongrass tops)
8 cups (1.75 liter) water
½ cup (100 g) sugar
1 tablespoon black tea or 2 black tea bags

1 Simmer the lemongrass and water over low heat for 20 minutes.
2 Remove from the heat, stir in the sugar and tea and steep for 20 minutes.
3 Strain, cool, and chill in the refrigerator. Serve over crushed ice.

Acknowledgments

The last two decades traveling through Thailand I have been honored to meet hundreds, if not thousands of talented cooks and chefs. I spend several months a year in Southeast Asia and without all my friends I have made travel would not be as easy, and I would certainly not learn as much about these dynamic food focused cultures. I thank each and every person that I have met along the way, each of you have formed the unique adventures I have been privileged to have experienced.

The idea for the book was sparked online. Social media has become an important part of my personal and business lives. Once I got hooked on Twitter (@chefdanhitweets) I met lots of really cool people, some even as obsessed with food as me. I discovered a blog Rasamalaysia.com that was founded, written, photographed and managed by the talented Bee Yinn Low, a Malaysian by birth, she and I hit it off immediately. She and her husband came over to cook a Malaysian Feast for a guest blog post and soon there after she introduced me to Eric Oey and Bud Sperry of Periplus Editions (Hong Kong) Ltd. Thanks Bee!

My next trip to Asia I met with Eric Oey of Periplus in Singapore at the always pleasant Grand Hyatt and having a long discussion and fabulous Thai meal prepared by David Thompson (more on him later). We both agreed to partner on this book, and for that he connected me to Bud Sperry, my editor. Bud was a pleasure to work with and as we passed recipes back and forth discussing the nuances of a recipes, I was able to develop all the recipes and the rest of my manuscript in less that 6 months. Thank you Bud for making my words flow, stories make sense, and grammar correct. I also appreciate the team that step into play at this stage of the publishing process, June Chong and Chan Sow Yun of Periplus Singapore office. Gail Tok and the marketing team from Periplus Singapore. A big thank you goes to the dynamic team of Christian Clements for food photography and Susie Donald for food styling, they were able to capture the essence of my recipes.

Writing a book is an arduous task, and one that is never the sole focus of your daily professional and personal life, it's something you fit into your already hectic life and the pressure it puts on your spouse is drastic. This was all handled with grace by my ever beautiful wife, Estrellita Leong-Danhi, whom most refer to as Esther. Now, more than two-decades of being a supportive spouse, business partner and best friend, I have her to thank for my success more than anyone else. Her hands on approach keeps our test kitchen running some days, and our household everyday. You are solely responsible for introducing me to Southeast Asia and that has helped me become who I am today. Thank you my love, I am forever grateful and cannot believe we made it through writing yet another book.

Get ready, you know another is coming soon.

Ari Slatkin my loyal Sous Chef for years stepped up to the plate again and was the main man on recipe testing for the entire book. Months of testing and retesting recipes he did not let up. I do appreciate all your intellectual and culinary contributions to all the work we do. Looking back at my test kitchen, for months stone mortar and pestles proudly sat next to gram scales and temperature probes as Brad Kent, the artesian pizza scientist and chef was occasionally called in to balance the workload and give me more time to cook every Thai recipe myself. Paul Foster, nearly twenty years of friendship and fellow chef once again jumped in and helped in the test kitchen as we juggled back and forth between recipe for this book and all the other culinary projects with my clients.

The amount of food that is used testing the recipes over and over was enormous, and fortunately I have friends at Melissa's World Variety Produce, especially Robert Schueller, the Director of Public Relations. He personally delivered incalculable pounds of aromatic lemongrass, various Asian greens, hands of ginger and galangal, bags of fiery red chilies, and even mangos by the case. They are always at the ready to provide me with building blocks of flavor around the country as I travel and teach about Southeast Asian Foods, a sincere thanks to you and all the team at Melissa's. With Thai food there is often Thai Singha Beer (at least with my meals) and Charles Chaicharee, Singha Beers' Director of Marketing Communications and Business Development has been very supportive when I do special events—kop khun maak kop for the bubbling malt!

A unique thanks goes out to those that have been my Thai achaan, teachers, as a fellow teacher I have a deep respect for you and the generosity you continue provide through educating people about your culture. I hope to continue your mission and bring the culinary foodways to the world. Khun Ning and Khun Kobkaew of Khao Cooking School, whom I first met in the USA and have cooked with in Thailand extensively. You are both some of the most gentle and talented people I know. Thank you for being not only my respected teachers also my dear friends. Thank you for introducing me to Chef David Thompson, whom I consider one of the great teachers of Thai food culture.

David has become my guiding light in my research on Thai food. While he was testing the recipes for his seminal mammoth picturesque book on Thai street food, I flew to Bangkok to cook with him, his sweet partner Tanongsak Yordwai and talented chef Jane Alty, a marathon of market visits, cutting, pounding, frying, boiling we created some amazing Thai food. Thank you for allowing me intimate access to your vast knowledge of Thai food, I have prevailed as a better cook. Many questions arose during the crafting of this book, he was always there with an answer. With deep gratitude, David, I look forward to a lifetime of learning and friendship.

Tik, you and your family welcomed me into your home and I will cherish that time forever, not to mention I still cook the Pumpkin and Pork with Scallions your lovely wife Gladporn Ongad taught me. Chiang Mai adventures with the first clean cut intellectual former monk and preppy Thai I have ever met, I look forward to

seeing you again soon! Some Thai folks have been instrumental in getting me access to the real Thai culture and am forever grateful. Fah Vorarittinapa, a former student of mine at the Culinary Institute of America (CIA) and now long time friend and her family in Thailand. Khun Aom, the bubbly Bangkokian as she likes to be called. Thank you for being my guide around Bangkok and being my translator on call and handling all those calls when I handed a phone to a Thai and asked you to solve the issue or answer a question.

Fortunately Thailand's government realizes the importance food plays in their culture and they have the business sense to support the Tourism Authority of Thailand (TAT) and all their efforts using food to lure people to the land of smiles. I have collaborated with the TAT for years and have been fortunate to have help and guidance from such champions of Thailand, especially Khun Charinee based with me here in Los Angeles, thanks to Khun Jamlong Ratanapan, Executive Director of TAT that guides the entire team I work with.

Within my consulting business, Chef Danhi & Co. (chefdanhi.com), we work with restaurants, food manufacturers and all sorts of professional associations and the Thailand's Department of Export Promotion (DEP) has been a big help, especially Executive Director, Khun Chantira Jimreivat Vivatrat who has created and launched several successful Thai Food Promotions, Deputy Director Chappon Rochanasena and Fon Duangporn for her Facebook prowess and help on all the projects. Congratulations goes to Chanchai Doungjit, the Director Western United States and Latin

America for managing these dynamic people.

Twenty-five years in the food business and I have too many people to thank than can be listed here. From my first job as a dishwasher to being an executive chef, the restaurant world is where I began. My alma mater, The Culinary Institute of America deserves a lifelong appreciation and thanks, the faculty and staff laid the foundation that I still stand on today. As a young culinarian you taught me that the culinary arts as a real profession and should be treated as such. Coming back to teach there for several years was a highlight of my career, a true honor and a immense learning opportunity, lessons I refer to daily. The CIA rocks!

A final thanks goes out to my family for putting up with my obsession with the cultures of Asia. My parents somehow took this New York born kid, raised me in Southern California and taught me that with a positive attitude, a solid education, ethical behavior and perseverance anything is possible. My siblings are all special people and all very successful in their own right, thanks for being there for me when I needed your emotional support and at times physical help.

The evolution of a book from idea to your hands involves hundred if not thousands of personalities and I hope I didn't miss any of these special people. Each person is a small piece of the complex puzzle, forgive me if I did not mention you, however you can be certain your influence can be tasted within the pages of this book, thanks.

Robert Danhi

Index

Resource Guide

Here are some of the books referenced while writing *Easy Thai Cooking*. The web has also become an amazing resource for recipes and Thai culture and some to help you find the ingredients that are the building blocks of flavor in this book. Make sure to check www.chefdanhi.com for updated information.

Books

- *Classic Thai Cuisine* by David Thompson
- *Dancing Shrimp* by Kasma Loha-Unchit
- *Encyclopedia of Asian Food* by Charmain Solomon
- *Essentials of Asian Cuisine* by Corinne Trang
- *Hot Sour Salty Sweet* by Naomi Duguid and Jeffrey Alford
- *It Rains Fishes* by Kasma Loha-Unchit
- *Savoring Southeast Asia* by Joyce Jue
- *South-East Asia* by Carl Withey
- *Southeast Asian Flavors* by Robert Danhi
- *Southeast Asian Food* by Rosemary Brissenden
- *Thai Cooking* by Carmack/Nabnian
- *Thai Curries Beyond Curries* by Chai Siriyarn
- *Thai Food* by David Thompson
- *Thai Street Food* by David Thompson
- *Thai, The Essence of Asian Cooking*
- *The Best of Thai Dishes* by Sisamon Kongpan
- *The Big Book of Thai Curries* by Vacharin Bhumichitr
- *The Food of Thailand*, Whitecap Publishing
- *The Original Thai Cookbook* by Jennifer Brennan
- *World Food Thailand* by Judy Williams

Web Resources for Ingredients

Melissa's for Produce and Dried Goods
    http://www.melissas.com/
Importfood.com for ingredients and equipment
    http://importfood.com
Temple of Thai for ingredients and equipment
    http://www.templeofthai.com
AMAZON for ingredients and equipment
    www.amazon.com
Asian Foods Online for ingredients and equipment
    www.asianfoodsonline.com

Web Resources for Thai Recipes and Cultural Information

Bee Yin's Easy Asian Recipes at
    www.rasamalaysia.com
Authentic Thai Food Culture at
    www.enjoythaifood.com
Great Cooking School on Koh Samui
    http://www.sitca.net/
Stories of Food, Travel and Life
    http://whiteonricecouple.com
Kasma Loha-unchit Thai Explorations
    www.thaifoodandtravel.com
Amazing Asian Food Blog EatingAsian
    http://eatingasia.typepad.com/
Tourism Authority of Thailand
    www.tourismthailand.org

Published by Tuttle Publishing, an imprint of Periplus Editions (HK) Ltd.

www.tuttlepublishing.com

Library of Congress Cataloging-in-Publication Data

Danhi, Robert.
  Easy Thai cooking : 75 simple recipes with authentic Thai flavors / by Robert Danhi ; foreword by Corinne Trang.
      p. cm.
  Includes bibliographical references and index.
  ISBN 978-0-8048-4179-5 (hardcover)
1. Cooking, Thai. 2. Cookbooks. I. Title.
  TX724.5.T5D36 2011
  641.59593--dc23
                              2011022777

ISBN 978-0-8048-4179-5

Distributed by
North America, Latin America & Europe
Tuttle Publishing
364 Innovation Drive, North Clarendon, VT 05759-9436 U.S.A.
Tel: 1 (802) 773-8930; Fax: 1 (802) 773-6993
info@tuttlepublishing.com; www.tuttlepublishing.com

Japan
Tuttle Publishing
Yaekari Building, 3rd Floor, 5-4-12 Osaki, Shinagawa-ku, Tokyo 141-0032
Tel: (81) 3 5437-0171; Fax: (81) 3 5437-0755
sales@tuttle.co.jp; www.tuttle.co.jp

Asia Pacific
Berkeley Books Pte. Ltd, 61 Tai Seng Avenue, #02-12, Singapore 534167
Tel: (65) 6280-1330, Fax: (65) 6280-6290
inquiries@periplus.com.sg; www.periplus.com

Printed in Hong Kong   1207EP
15 14 13 12   6 5 4 3 2

TUTTLE PUBLISHING® is a registered trademark of Tuttle Publishing, a division of Periplus Editions (HK) Ltd.

The Tuttle Story: "Books to Span the East and West"

Most people are surprised to learn that the world's largest publisher of books on Asia had its humble beginnings in the tiny American state of Vermont. The company's founder, Charles Tuttle, came from a New England family steeped in publishing, and his first love was books—especially old and rare editions.

Tuttle's father was a noted antiquarian dealer in Rutland, Vermont. Young Charles honed his knowledge of the trade working in the family bookstore, and later in the rare books section of Columbia University Library. His passion for beautiful books—old and new—never wavered through his long career as a bookseller and publisher.

After graduating from Harvard, Tuttle enlisted in the military and in 1945 was sent to Tokyo to work on General Douglas MacArthur's staff. He was tasked with helping to revive the Japanese publishing industry, which had been utterly devastated by the war. When his tour of duty was completed, he left the military, married a talented and beautiful singer, Reiko Chiba, and in 1948 began several successful business ventures.

To his astonishment, Tuttle discovered that postwar Tokyo was actually a book-lover's paradise. He befriended dealers in the Kanda district and began supplying rare Japanese editions to American libraries. He also imported American books to sell to the thousands of GIs stationed in Japan. By 1949, Tuttle's business was thriving, and he opened Tokyo's very first English-language bookstore in the Takashimaya Department Store in Ginza, to great success. Two years later, he began publishing books to fulfill the growing interest of foreigners in all things Asian.

Though a westerner, Tuttle was hugely instrumental in bringing a knowledge of Japan and Asia to a world hungry for information about the East. By the time of his death in 1993, he had published over 6,000 books on Asian culture, history and art—a legacy honored by Emperor Hirohito in 1983 with the "Order of the Sacred Treasure," the highest honor Japan bestows upon non-Japanese.

The Tuttle company today maintains an active backlist of some 1,500 titles, many of which have been continuously in print since the 1950s and 1960s—a great testament to Charles Tuttle's skill as a publisher. More than 60 years after its founding, Tuttle Publishing is more active today than at any time in its history, still inspired by Charles Tuttle's core mission—to publish fine books to span the East and West and provide a greater understanding of each.